CW01651692

Absolutely Delicious

Introduction

Many have asked for another recipe book to follow 'Simply Delicious'. Well here it is! Those of you who bought the first recipe book will be delighted to hear that well over £9000 has so far been raised from the sales of the book, for MS Research at The National Hospital for Neurology and Neurosurgery.

In a recent independent review, studies undertaken by research teams at the National Hospital were rated as leading the world and money raised from Absolutely Delicious will be used to aid that research.

A full range of services is provided for MS patients at the hospital, some of whom may only be in their twenties. New methods for assessment and monitoring disease progress are being developed and new drugs are being trialed which decrease the frequency of relapses. Comprehensive management of the disease is planned with other hospital departments, such as neurohabilitation, uro–neurology and pain relief.

Special thanks are again due to the girls of Ashford School who have typeset the recipes and those who have provided the illustrations (especially Nadia Husain). Thanks are also due to Lesley Pargeter and Geoff Gould (members of staff at Ashford School) who have spent innumerable hours in laying out the pages.

Of course the greatest thanks ought to be to Sally Gow who has been a great inspiration and without whose hard work the book would not have been possible.

We hope that you enjoy the recipes and thank you for buying the book, thereby contributing to a very worthy cause. To help you find your way around the book, please make use of the specially prepared index at the back.

If you would like to obtain further copies of the book, please contact Sally Gow, c/o Ashford School, East Hill, Ashford, Kent TN24 8PB.

The National Hospital
for Neurology and Neurosurgery
Development Foundation

The National Hospital
Queen Square, London
WC1N 3BG

Telephone 0171 829 8724
Fax 0171 278 2252

President

John Young CBE

Chairman

Michael Stone

Deputy Chairman

Marquess of Tavistock DL

Trustees

Alan Crockard FRCS
Edward Datnow FRCS
Professor George du Boulay CBE
Neil Edmonstone
Peter Foster
Professor Richard Frackowiak FRCS
Howard Guard
Frank Harding CA
Professor Ian McDonald FRCS
Professor David Marsden FRS
Harry Salmon
Christopher Sporborg
Alan Stubbs BDS
Patrick Vaughan
Andrew Wates

Director

Paul Meyer

Registered Charity
number 290173

A limited company
registered in England
number 1844281

Dear Supporter

It is a great pleasure to write the forward for Absolutely Delicious.

This book contains many interesting and unusual recipes which I hope you will have fun creating. At the same time you will have the pleasure of knowing that that dish has, in its own way, supported the multiple sclerosis research work of The National Hospital.

Both the hospital and I are indebted to Sally Gow and to Ashford School for their enthusiastic work in putting together this book. Their efforts and your purchase, will help us to continue our pioneering work.

Bon Appetit!

Michael Stone
CHAIRMAN

Contents

Chapter 1

Starters

Sopade Ajo

Serves 4

12 cloves garlic
3 cans water
1 heaped tsp cumin seed
6 tbsp olive oil
1 bayleaf
Salt to taste
2 cans Campbells consommé
6 x ½¨ slices stale french bread
1 heaped tsp paprika
1 Chorizo Spanish spiced sausage
½ cup dry sherry

Peel and thinly slice garlic and cook gently in oil (don't brown) in a heavy bottom pan. Cut chorizo into small cubes and cook with garlic. Then strain garlic and chorizo and return oil to pan. Break up bread and fry until all the oil is absorbed. Return chorizo and garlic, add consommé and three cans of water and add the bayleaf, paprika and cumin. Simmer for about half an hour. Just before serving, add sherry. For a more substantial dish you could poach four eggs in the soup.

David Gow
Kent

Potiron Soup

2 lb pumpkin * or 1 citroville
2 potatoes
2 onions
Sugar to taste
4 - 5 tomatoes
2 cloves garlic
Salt and pepper
1½ pints chicken stock

Cut pumpkin into bite sized pieces, skin and chop tomatoes, peel and chop potatoes, onions and cloves of garlic. Put all ingredients into a large saucepan and cook gently until vegetables are soft. Liquidise until smooth and check seasoning. This soup should be quite thick and sweet. Serve with a good spoonful of cream and croûtons fried in butter and mixed herbs.

* Pumpkin is larger and not as sweet as "citroville", a deep orange in colour and the size of a melon. This soup is really delicious when made with citroville.

Mrs Peter Alliott
Normandy, France

Onion Cream Soup

4 large onions
2 pt chicken stock
3 egg yolks
Grated Gruyère
2 oz butter
¼ to ⅜ pt double cream
Salt and pepper

Peel the onions and cut them into thin slices. Melt the butter in a thick pan, add the onions and cook them gently till soft. Add the stock, bring to the boil and simmer steadily for about half an hour. Liquidise, season and bring to the boil again. Stir the cream, beaten up with the egg yolks into a little of the soup left in the pan, season well and reheat without boiling. Serve with a big bowl of Gruyère cheese. This is such a simple recipe that the combination of flavours must be perfect - if you can't get Gruyère, Emmenthal will do. Serve with hot toast.

Mrs James Woodhouse
Kent

French Onion Soufflé Soup

1 large onion
15 g flour
125 ml milk
1 egg - separated
1 tbsp brandy
750 ml good brown stock
15 g butter
25 g cheese - finely grated
4 slices of french bread - toasted

1. Peel and thinly slice the onion in rings. Simmer gently in the stock until tender.
2. Meanwhile, make a thick sauce with butter, flour and milk - cool and beat in egg yolk and cheese.
3. Whisk the egg white until stiff and fold into the mixture.
4. Add the brandy to the soup and pour into 4 heated bowls. Float a slice of toasted french bread on top and divide the soufflé mixture between the 4 bowls.
5. Stand on a baking sheet and bake at 210°C / gas 7 for approx 20 minutes or until soufflé is golden brown and puffy. Serve immediately.

Ginny Lingwood
Ashford School

Courgette and Dill Soup

1 lb courgettes
1 oz butter
1 pt chicken / vegetable stock
Fresh pre-packed dill or equivalent
1 medium onion or 4 spring onions
Salt and pepper
¼ pt double cream
2 potatoes

1. Roughly chop the courgettes, onions and potatoes.
2. Sauté lightly in butter until the onions are translucent.
3. Add the stock.
4. Cook until all the ingredients are tender.
5. Leave to cool.
6. Liquidize or blend, adding the dill, until smooth.
7. Gently re-heat. Dilute with water if necessary.
8. Add the cream prior to serving.
9. Serve with a small sprig of fresh dill.

Henrietta Laitt
London

Welsh Onion Soup

Serves 2

Peel and slice about 12 oz of onions very thinly. Boil them to a pulp in water to cover. Then stir in 4 oz of grated Cheddar cheese, a good dessertspoon of butter and salt and pepper to taste. Mix it well. Then add half a pint of milk and heat, stirring, until it almost boils.

Princess Juliet Melikoff
London

Carrot and Tomato Soup

2 lb carrots
450 ml tin tomatoes
4 oz butter
Salt and pepper
Parsley
1 large onion
4 cups chicken stock
Pinch of sugar
½ cup cream (optional)

Chop onion and carrots and fry in butter for 10 minutes. Add the tin of tomatoes and the stock. Simmer for 45 minutes. Cool. Then put through Wizz or liquidise. Add the cream. Serve with parsley.

I grate or slice the carrots in the Wizz and also the onion. I also fry the onion first and do the carrots in two pans as there always seems to be rather a lot. All very quick and easy. Feeds plenty.

Sarah Walker
Argyllshire

Broccoli and Stilton Soup

12 oz broccoli
2 oz Stilton cheese
Black pepper
Chicken stock (or chicken cube and water)

Cut broccoli into pieces. Place into a saucepan, cover with stock, or water and chicken cube. Simmer until broccoli is tender. Take off heat and add Stilton. Put into liquidiser and liquidise. Reheat and add pepper to taste.

Mrs Jenny Ursell
Kent

Cold Creamed Carrot and Orange Soup

1½ lb (720 g) carrots
2 oz (60 g) soft margarine
3 oranges
3 medium onions
2 pt (1.2 litres) chicken stock
¼ pt (150 ml) cream
Fresh parsley
Seasoning

Melt the butter and sauté the sliced carrot and the onions without browning. Add the stock, seasoning and simmer for about half an hour until the carrots are cooked. Cool and then liquidize. When cold add the juice of 2 oranges and as much of the third as required, to taste. Chill. Before serving add the cream and chopped parsley.

Mrs Peter Stevens
Kent

Caviar Mousse

Serves 8

3 medium jars black lumpfish
8 fl oz (250 ml) double cream
3 spring onions finely chopped
1 glass vodka (optional)
2 tablespoons mayonnaise
1 sachet powdered gelatine
Seasoning

Dissolve the gelatine in a little warm water, and add to the other ingredients, mixing well. Place in a mould and leave in fridge for 2 - 3 hours to set. Before serving remove from mould, decorate with slices of lemon and serve with toast.

Mrs Ian Johnston
Kent

Smoked Haddock and Avocado au Gratin

Serves 4-6

½ lb smoked haddock
1 oz butter
Pepper and mace
1 - 2 avocados (depending on size)
1 oz flour
1 bay leaf
½ pt creamy milk (use top of the milk or add a little cream)
6 - 8 tbsp grated Gruyère or mature Cheddar cheese

Place the skinned fish in a saucepan with the bay leaf and milk, bring gently to the simmer and draw to the side of the stove; cover and leave for 5 - 10 minutes (the fish will then be cooked). Melt the butter in another saucepan, add the flour and cook for 2 - 3 minutes over moderate heat. Draw off the stove, wait for the sizzling to cease (make sure it does, as you are adding hot liquid), and add the strained milk from the fish. Whisk with wire whisk and bring to the boil. Simmer for 1 - 2 minutes, fold in the flaked fish, and season with pepper and mace, adding salt only if necessary. Spoon into individual ramekins, top with slices of peeled avocado, sprinkle heavily with cheese and grill until brown and bubbling.

Mrs Michael Drummond-Brady
Kent

Smoked Haddock Mousse

8 oz smoked haddock
¼ pt mayonnaise
¼ pt chicken stock
¾ pt béchamel sauce
½ oz gelatine
½ pt double cream - whipped lightly
Salt and pepper
Garnish - hard boiled egg and chopped parsley

1. Cook haddock, skin and flake.
2. Mix béchamel sauce and mayonnaise together.
3. Soak gelatine in stock, melt and add to sauce.
4. Stir in haddock.
5. When thickening, stir in whipped cream. Season.
6. Turn into a 6" souffle dish or individual ramekins. Allow to set. Chill.
7. Garnish with slices of hard boiled egg and parsley.

Mrs John Martin
Kent

Marinated Salmon (raw!)

Serves 6 - 8 as a first course

1½ lb middle cut salmon
¼ pt walnut or sunflower oil
1 clove garlic - finely chopped
1 glass dry white wine
1 shallot - peeled and sliced
2 tsp sea salt
Ground pepper
Juice and thinly chopped rind of 1½ lemons and 1½ oranges

1. Remove skin from salmon and cut flesh neatly from both sides of bone, or get the fishmonger to remove the backbone for you!
2. Remove any bones with tweezers and cut into fillets about 1½ inches thick.
3. Place the fillets into a shallow dish. Mix all the other ingredients together and pour over the fish.
4. Cover and refrigerate for 10 - 12 hours - turns a sort of opaque colour.

Good with a walnut and celery salad.

Vivien Owston
Kent

Toasted Muffins with Smoked Salmon

Muffins
Sour cream
Salmon eggs or mock caviar
Smoked salmon
Dill sauce
Dill for decoration

Toast muffins. When still warm spread with dill sauce, pile on the smoked salmon, a blob of sour cream and top with either salmon eggs or mock caviar. Decorate with a sprig of dill.

Mrs Angela Straker
Perthshire

Sauce for Oysters

2 shallots, very finely chopped
Parsley, very finely chopped
2 tbsp white wine vinegar
1 tbsp sweet sherry
2 cloves garlic, very finely chopped
Few dashes Tabasco
2 tbsp olive oil

Mix all the above ingredients and add about half a teaspoon to each oyster just before eating. Sauce improves if kept in refrigerator for 24 hours.

Charlie Alliott
Tokyo

Prawn and Tomato Ramekins

Serves 6

1 oz onion - chopped
1 tbsp flour
1 tsp tomato purée
Freshly ground black pepper
1 oz Parmesan cheese - grated
1 garlic clove - peeled and crushed
8 oz can tomatoes
Salt
8 oz peeled prawns
1 oz fresh white breadcrumbs

Melt butter in a pan, add the onion and garlic and fry gently until soft. Stir in the flour, then the tomatoes, tomato purée and salt and pepper to taste. Simmer for 20 minutes. Work through a sieve and mix with prawns. Spoon the mixture into 6 individual freezer-proof ramekins or oven-proof dishes, smooth

the tops and sprinkle with the cheese and breadcrumbs.
To freeze - Open freeze, then wrap in foil, seal and label.

To serve - Remove wrappings and thaw at room temperature for two hours. Reheat in a preheated oven 180°C / 350°F / gas 4 for 20 minutes or until heated through and golden brown on top.

Mrs Daphne Lott
Kent

Avocado Grilled with Prawns

Avocados
Cheese (Cheddar of Gruyère)
Prawns
Mayonnaise

Halve avocados. Fill with layers of prawns and mayonnaise and some cheese, sliced or grated. Grill 3" from element. (I have used ordinary Cheddar but Gruyère is recommended.)

Judy Canney
Kent

Avocados Stuffed with Crab

Serves 4

2 ripe avocados
1 dessert apple
3 tbsp mayonnaise
Salt and pepper
Cream
170 g / 6 oz white crab meat
1 stick celery
1 tsp finely grated lemon rind
French dressing or oil

Split the avocados, remove the stones and immediately brush the cut surface with french dressing or oil to prevent them discolouring. Sort through the crab meat to remove any pieces of inedible cartilage and peel and chop the apple and celery with mayonnaise lightened by the addition of a little cream and grated lemon rind. Season with salt and pepper to taste, and pile into the avocado halves.

Mrs Jane Horne
Kent

Sardine Paté

2 oz butter
Juice ½ lemon
4 oz can sardines in oil
3 oz soft breadcrumbs (brown or white)
1 tbsp chopped parsley
Ground black pepper

Melt butter, remove from heat, stir in breadcrumbs and remaining ingredients. Beat until smooth, season to taste, chill until firm. Garnish with lemon wedges and olives. Serve with melba toast.

Ann Cooper
Essex

Mrs Kerrigan's Hot Chicken Salad

One chicken breast per person
Lettuce
Lemon juice
One rasher bacon per person
Olive oil
Salt and pepper

Heat a little oil in a frying pan and fry the bacon until crisp. Remove, crumble and keep warm. Now fry the chicken which has been cut into thin slivers. When nearly cooked, return the bacon, add a tablespoon or two of lemon juice and salt and pepper to taste. While the bacon and chicken are cooking, prepare a bed of lettuce on each plate. When the chicken and bacon have heated through, pour over the bed of lettuce on each plate, together with the juices from the pan. Add extra french dressing if needed. This is extra specially delicious if you add a few slices of avocado to each plate of salad.

Anonymous

Chicken Liver Tartlets

1 tub (8 oz) frozen chicken livers
¾ lb green grapes (halved and seeded)
Garlic if desired
½ pt stock
¾ lb mushrooms
3 tbsp home made tomato sauce
Nutmeg, thyme and parsley
4 small cooked individual quiche type tartlets, (lined with short crust pastry)

In a frying pan, cook the mushrooms in butter and add to stock with nutmeg and thyme. Add livers, halving any large ones. When cooked, add tomato sauce. Divide mixture between pastry shells decorating with grapes and parsley.

Mrs Angela Straker
Perthshire

Chicken Liver and Roquefort Salad

Serves 4

½ lb chicken livers
Olive oil
Salt and pepper
Green salad using lettuce, radicchio, endive, watercress, chicory
¼ lb Roquefort cheese
Lemon juice

Clean and trim the livers, carefully removing any greenish parts and the sinews. Dry the livers in paper towels, slicing the larger pieces in two. Cut the cheese into cubes. Toss the salad vegetables in oil, salt, pepper and lemon juice and add the chunks of cheese. Arrange on individual plates.

Put a few drops of oil in the frying pan, enough to stop the meat from sticking and when smoking, fry all the liver for two or three minutes, shaking the pan a few times, not stirring as this tends to break them up. When ready - that is, still slightly pink in the middle when you stick a knife point in - place the liver pieces on top of the salad, pour on any pan juices and serve while still warm.

Mrs Vyvyan Harmsworth
Kent

Chicken Liver Paté

½ lb chicken livers
Butter
2 shallots, finely sliced
Cognac

Melt a large knob of butter in a frying pan and gently soften the shallots. Add chicken livers and cook until browned on outside but still pink inside. Season with salt and pepper. Place in liquidiser, add a good splash of cognac and liquidise until smooth. Pour into container. Melt butter in a pan and pour on top of paté. Cool in refrigerator.

Mrs Peter Alliott
Normandy, France

Curried Egg Paté

Serves 4 as a small starter

2 hard boiled eggs
1 tsp curry powder
2 dstsp Hellmans mayonnaise
1 oz melted butter

Chop eggs and mash finely, mix with mayonnaise and curry powder, then add melted butter and season with salt and pepper if wanted. Press into dish or small bowl and allow to set. Serve paté with toast or in a nest of cress or watercress and eat with a fork.

Mary Blaksley
Herts

Egg Mousse

5 hard boiled eggs
Salt and pepper
Worcester sauce
½ pint whipped cream
Pinch paprika
Anchovy sauce to taste
Harvey sauce, if you have it
4 tbsp stiff aspic (made and allowed to nearly set)

Sieve the egg yolks and chop the whites. Mix all the seasonings with sieved yolks. You should have quite a strong tasting mixture as the whites and cream absorb flavour. Add the aspic (I usually make up a pint of aspic and use 4 good tablespoons in the mousse, and the rest mashed up on the top for decoration when set). When mixture is beginning to set, add the lightly whipped cream and lastly the chopped whites. Pour into a soufflé dish and chill. Decorate with chopped aspic and chopped parsley.

Anne Findlay
Kent

Quails Egg Tartlets

Serves 4

4 sheets filo pastry
1½ oz butter
1 tbsp cream
1 tbsp olive oil
¼ pint milk
1 tbsp Parmesan

1 tbsp Cheddar cheese
8 oz flat mushrooms
8 oz baking beans
1 tsp plain flour
8 quails eggs
4 x 8 - 10 cm tartlet moulds

A. Make the tartlets:

1. Take the filo pastry and cut each into 4 equal pieces.
2. Melt butter, add oil and layer the 4 pieces into the mould lightly brushing with butter mix and tidy up the edges where the pastry overhangs.
3. Put some baking beans in the middle and bake for 10 - 15 minutes until golden. Allow to cool before removing beans.

B. Soft boil the eggs:

Cover with cold water in a saucepan, bring to the boil, take off the heat, leave for 30 seconds then plunge into cold water and shell when cold.

C. Make the duxelle:

Finely chop or mince the mushrooms and add to ½ oz melted butter in a saucepan. Cook on low heat until liquid evaporated - season with salt and pepper.

D. Make the mornay sauce:

Melt ½ oz butter, add 1 teaspoon flour then stir in milk, cream and cheese. Cook on low heat for 10 minutes stirring regularly. Season with salt and pepper.

E. Assembly:

1. Put a teaspoon of duxelle in each tartlet and warm in the oven for 5 minutes.
2. Drop the eggs into a pan of boiling water for 30 seconds and place on top of the duxelle.
3. Spoon the warmed mornay sauce over the top, put onto a plate garnished with endive lettuce and radiccio and serve.

HRH The Princess of Wales

Uncle Bob's Breakfast

Quails, 1 per person
Lemon juice
Croûtons of french bread
Chicken liver paté
Butter

Many years ago an uncle was asked what he would like for breakfast. "What I'd like is a cold partridge and a bottle of claret, but what I'll get is the usual boring bowl of cornflakes and two pieces of toast!"

Ever since, we have started Christmas Day with a breakfast of cold partridge and claret, until, that is, this Christmas, when partridges were unobtainable here, so I devised a similar feast.

Cut a piece of crusty french bread for each bird and spread generously with paté and butter. Put quail on slices of bread and place on baking tray. Dot with butter and a squeeze of lemon. Put in preheated oven at 160°C for 40 minutes or until juices just run clear. When cooked, leave to cool but do not refrigerate.

Mrs Peter Alliott
Normandy, France

My Starter

Melon balls
Diced avocado
Crisp lettuce
Mayonnaise
Sections of pink grapefruit
Prawns
Red lettuce
Heinz tomato sauce

Make a french dressing and marinade grapefruit sections. Drain well. Add a little Heinz tomato sauce, cream and a few drops of lemon juice to mayonnaise. Assemble everything at last moment and pour mayonnaise over pink grapefruit. Serve in individual glass dishes garnished with whole prawns.

Mrs Reg Older
Kent

Cottage Cheese Salad

Serves 2

2 celery stalks
½ 1b cottage cheese
½ tsp Worcestershire sauce
1 bunch watercress
Salt and freshly ground pepper
2 spring onions
1 tsp chopped red or green peppers
2 drops Tabasco sauce
Paprika pepper

Finely chop the celery. Very thinly slice the spring onions. Combine the cottage cheese with the pepper, celery and spring onions and mix in the Worcestershire sauce and the Tabasco. Season with salt and pepper and arrange the salad on a bed of watercress leaves dipped into french dressing. Sprinkle the cheese with a little paprika and chill before serving.

Anonymous

Twice Baked Cheese Soufflé

½ pint milk with a slice of onion and a pinch of nutmeg
2 oz butter
Pinch mustard
4 eggs
2 oz flour
4½ oz grated cheese
12 oz single cream

Heat the milk. Melt the butter and add the flour. Add the heated, strained milk to make the white sauce. Boil for a few minutes. Add the grated cheese and mustard. Beat in the egg yolks one by one. Whisk egg whites until stiff but not dry, fold in thoroughly. Fill oiled ramekins half full. Bake in bain-marie in oven at 350°F / 180°C / gas 4 for 15 minutes until well risen and brown. Remove from oven, allow to cool and sink. This can be done in advance. Turn out and place in ovenproof dish for serving. Ten minutes before required, mix 1½ oz cheese with the seasoned cream and spread or pour onto soufflé. Return to oven for 10 minutes at 450°F / 230°C.

Ann Faulkner
Yorkshire

Spinach Roulade

Roulade:

1 lb frozen spinach purée
4 eggs, separated
Freshly grated nutmeg
1 oz butter
Salt and freshly ground black pepper
4 - 6 tbsp grated Parmesan cheese

Sauce:

1½ oz butter
1 oz plain flour
¾ pt milk
Salt and cayenne pepper
6 oz button mushrooms, chopped
½ oz cornflour
1 oz grated Cheddar

Preheat the oven to 190°C / 375°F / gas 5.

Line an 8 x 12 inch Swiss roll tin with non-stick paper, greased with oil or butter and sprinkled with half the Parmesan cheese.

Make the sauce by melting the butter in a pan and gently frying the mushrooms for 3 - 4 minutes. Remove from the pan with a slotted spoon and set aside. Stir the flour into the butter remaining in the pan, and cook for 2 - 3 minutes, then remove from the heat. Blend the cornflour with the milk, and gradually stir it into the pan, mixing well. Bring the sauce to the boil, and simmer it for 2 - 3 minutes. Remove from the heat and add the grated Cheddar, salt and cayenne pepper to taste.

Squeeze as much water as you can from the spinach. Then put it into a saucepan with the butter and cook gently until heated through. Remove the saucepan from the heat and add the egg yolks, mixing them in thoroughly. Whisk the egg whites until stiff but not dry and fold them into the spinach. Season with salt, pepper and nutmeg.

Pour the mixture into the tin, smoothing it into the corners. Bake for about 15 - 20 minutes, until set and golden brown on the surface. Remove from the oven and invert it onto a wire tray covered with a piece of clean greaseproof paper. Peel away the lining paper and leave the roulade to cool slightly. Spread the sauce evenly over the surface and roll up the roulade like a swiss roll. Sprinkle the top with the rest of the Parmesan cheese. Then heat through in the oven before serving.

This is ideal to keep frozen in the freezer for those unexpected vegetarian visitors, as you can hack a slice off and keep the rest for later, or if using the whole thing, after it has completely thawed, place it on a baking sheet in a preheated oven at 180°C / 350°F / gas 4 for 20 - 30 minutes to heat right through.

Mrs Richard Jenkins
Cambridgeshire

Avocados in Spinach Jelly with Garlic and Chilli

Serves 6

¾ pt water
5 spinach leaves, chopped roughly
4 tsp caster sugar
2 tbsp white wine vinegar
3 tsp powdered gelatine
3 - 4 pinches chilli powder
3 garlic cloves, chopped roughly
3 avocados
Juice of 1 lemon
Fresh dill to garnish

Put the water, chilli powder, chopped spinach, garlic, sugar and a good sprinkling of salt into a saucepan. Bring to the boil, then simmer gently for 10 minutes. Cut the avocados in half lengthways. Remove stones and peel off the skin carefully. Cut the avocados fairly thinly crossways and put in a bowl sprinkling them with the white wine vinegar as you go, to prevent them discolouring. Then arrange the slices in layers in a 2 pint glass serving dish. Remove the spinach mixture from the heat and sprinkle in the gelatine making sure it has thoroughly dissolved. Stir in the lemon juice. Strain the liquid through a sieve into a jug discarding any spinach or garlic left in the sieve. Pour the strained liquid over the avocados slowly so that it seeps right to the bottom. Leave the jelly to cool and then refrigerate for at least 3 hours. Garnish with the dill.

Sara Hurst
London

Spinach with Herbs and Cream

750 g chopped spinach
200 g ham, diced (cooked)
200 g grated Cheddar
1½ tsp dried tarragon
1 clove garlic, crushed
2 large eggs
150 ml double cream
2 tsp chervil

Thaw spinach and drain. Mix with the rest of the ingredients. Put in a greased ovenproof dish and cook 200 - 225°C for 25 - 30 minutes. Serve with nice bread and a salad. (Ideal for lunch or a light supper.)

Mrs Miles Dorman
Hampshire

Artichoke Starter

1 tin globe artichokes (drained)
4 rashers streaky bacon
Chopped walnuts
Lettuce leaf hearts
200 g light Philadelphia cheese
Thick, sliced bread
King prawns

Fry rounds of thick sliced bread (large pastry cutter) and dry on paper towel. Fry four rashers of streaky bacon and chop up finely. Mix in with the artichoke and cheese which has been whisked in a Magimix When cold, put the rounds of fried bread on a plate and top with artichoke mixture. Sprinkle with chopped walnuts, decorate with king prawns and serve on lettuce leaf hearts.

Mrs Tom Harris
Kent

Asparagus Mousse

Serves 4

1 tbsp double cream, lightly whipped
3 oz cream cheese (Philadelphia)
1 large cup asparagus purée
1 tbsp mayonnaise
½ packet gelatine
1 egg white beaten till stiff

Save a few asparagus tips to garnish. Beat the cheese till softened then add cream, mayonnaise and purée. Melt the gelatine in a little water over hot water and add to mixture. Fold in beaten egg white and pour into four ramekins. Keep in the fridge till required.

Mrs Reg Older
Kent

Yoghurt Mousse

Blend 1 can of consommé with 1 small carton of natural yoghurt, 1 clove of garlic and a pinch of cayenne pepper. Leave in the fridge to set. Garnish with a sprinkle of paprika pepper and black olives. Good for calorie counters.

Pat Silvester
Devon

Baked Chicory

Serves 4

8 chicory
3 oz butter, cut into knobs
1 handful of breadcrumbs
Lemon quarters
2 handfuls of grated Parmesan, Provelone or Gruyère
2 oz prosciutto / smoked ham, chopped
Salt and pepper
2 tbsp chopped parsley

Preheat the oven to 190°C / 375°F / gas 5. Remove any discoloured leaves from the chicory. Cut lengthways and arrange in a tightly fitting layer in a well-buttered gratin dish, split side down with the prosciutto and half the butter arranged between them. Sprinkle with salt and pepper and cover with tin foil. Place in the top half of the oven and bake for 45 minutes. Combine the cheese, parsley and breadcrumbs. Remove the chicory form the oven and turn it up to 220°C / 425°F / gas 7. Discard the tin foil, sprinkle the breadcrumb mixture on top, dot with butter and return to the highest shelf in the oven until brown and bubbling (5 - 10 minutes).

Serve with the lemon quarters, bread and a green salad.

Princess Juliet Melikoff
London

A Spicy Starter

Serves 2

This makes a wonderful starter or a light supper dish served with a hot crusty roll. You can put in anything that takes your fancy, use up leftovers if you have them. Typically this is what I do.

Butter two heat-proof individual oven-to-table baking dishes approximately 5" diameter by 1" depth (ramekins are too small and deep for this). Place in each of the dishes in separate little piles leaving a slight dip in the centre

1 tbsp thinly sliced cooked chicken
1 tbsp thinly sliced cooked ham
1 tbsp cooked chopped onion
1 tbsp sliced mushroom cooked in butter
1 tbsp cooked green vegetable eg spinach or broccoli
1 tbsp cooked peas
1 teaspoon sun dried tomato from a jar
1 tbsp white sauce over the mushrooms
1 tbsp salsa sauce (this is essential)
1 or 2 sliced black olives

Now, either break a whole egg and slide gently over the whole keeping the yolk in the centre dip or beat the egg and pour over the whole. Season with a very little salt and some freshly milled black pepper. Bake at the top of a hot oven for about five minutes or until the egg has cooked to your taste and serve immediately.

Alex Palmer
Ashford School

Mushroom Starter

Mushrooms, 2 oz per person
Small onion or shallot
Fresh (or dried) thyme or garlic
Lemon juice
Bread, half a slice per person
Butter, flour and milk
Salt and pepper
Fried breadcrumbs

Soften the finely chopped onion in some butter and then add the finely chopped mushrooms till they are cooked. Thicken the juices with a little flour and cook, adding a little milk to make a sauce. Season with salt and freshly ground pepper, add lemon juice and chopped thyme to taste. Divide the mixture into ramekin dishes and top with crisply fried breadcrumbs.

Finely chopped or crumbled crispy grilled streaky bacon (half a rasher per person) and garlic are also delicious, instead of the lemon and thyme. Crushed crisps are a quick substitute for the fried crumbs as a topping. Everything can be prepared in advance: just add crumbs on top of the mushrooms at the last minute and heat through (oven or microwave).

Mrs Richard Boddington
Somerset

Smokey's Magic Mushrooms

Serves 4

4 slices bread
2 oz butter
½ lb mushrooms, sliced
Chopped parsley

Using a pastry cutter, cut out circles of the bread and butter both the sides of bread. Place bread on a baking sheet. Crush garlic and sauté in the butter with the sliced mushrooms and when al denté, stir in the parsley. Heap piles of the garlic mushrooms into the centre of the bread and pop it in the oven for 5 - 10 minutes, until the bread has turned into fried bread. Delicious.

Exactly the same can be done substituting the mushrooms with onions and a tin of tomatoes, (these you cook for a long time until they go gluggy and scrumptious). Pile on top of the circles of bread and they are wonderful. Both these can be reduced in size for eats with drinks, but I am greedy and love them as a first course and sometimes I do the tomato ones with just a salad for lunch parties.

Mrs David Spry
Kent

Fruited Couscous Salad with Coriander and Ginger

175 g (6 oz) couscous
Finely grated zest and juice of 1 lime
3 - 4 tbsp rice or cider vinegar
25 g (1 oz) currants
Salt and pepper
3 - 4 tbsp fresh coriander
120 ml (4 fl oz) orange juice
4 tbsp olive oil
50 g (2 oz) dried apricots, chopped
2.5 cm (1") piece fresh ginger, grated
1 small red onion, chopped
2 tbsp toasted pine kernels

1. Place couscous in a large bowl. In a small bowl mix orange juice, lime juice and olive oil with two tablespoons vinegar, and add 150 ml (¼ pt) boiling water.
2. Pour liquids over couscous, fork through and leave to stand for 30 minutes.
3. Place chopped onion in a sieve and pour over boiling water, drain and toss in a bowl with a little remaining vinegar.
4. When the couscous has absorbed all the liquid, fluff it up with a fork and stir in the onion, coriander and pine kernels. Add more salt to taste, and season well with pepper.

Eastbourne College of Food and Fashion
Rannies

Devilled Chestnut Bites

For each skewer - serve one or two per person

2 slices streaky bacon (rinds removed)
4 peeled, cooked chestnuts (or tinned)
½ tsp Dijon mustard
2 frozen chicken livers
1 tbsp Worcestershire sauce

Stretch bacon slices and cut in half. While chicken livers are still quite solid, cut in half and wrap bacon around them. Thread onto wooden skewers, alternating with the chestnuts. Mix mustard and Worcestershire sauce together and spread over the kebabs. Grill, turning frequently, until bacon is crisp, and serve hot.

Mrs Michel Gatenby
London

Chapter 2

This And That

Staffordshire Oatcakes

Makes approximately 12 oatcakes

8 oz fine or medium oatmeal
1 tsp salt
1½ pts warm milk and water (mixed)
8 oz strong plain white flour
1½ tsp dried instant yeast

1. Add salt to flour and oatmeal and stir.
2. Stir in dried yeast.
3. Mix dry ingredients with warm liquid to make a nice batter.
4. Cover with clean cloth and leave in a warm place for about 1 hour.
5. Bake on a well greased bakestone, griddle or thick based frying pan. Turn each oatcake after 2 to 3 minutes when upper side appears dry and underside will be golden brown and bake for a further 2 to 3 minutes.

To serve: Fry with bacon and eggs for breakfast or tea, or grill and eat hot with butter.

These will keep for several days in a polythene bag in a refrigerator. They also freeze well. Put paper or polythene tissue between each oatcake. May be taken straight from freezer into frying pan.

Anne Gould
Ashford School

Stilton Paté with Garlic Bread

½ lb Stilton
1 fl oz milk
1 oz walnuts, chopped
4 oz soft butter
Crushed garlic
1 dstsp fresh cream
8 oz cream cheese
1 small crusty loaf white bread
2 tsp mixed herbs

For the paté:

Blend Stilton cheese with cream and milk. Blend in cream cheese and walnuts. Pile into serving dish.

For the bread:

Slice loaf into half inch slices to within half inch of the base. Mash butter and herbs together with garlic. Spread both sides of the bread with butter. Wrap in foil and bake for 15 - 20 minutes at 375°F / 190°C / gas 5.

Mrs John Martin
Kent

Mini Curry Puffs (popular with drinks)

Puff or short crust pastry

Make up your own recipe curry with minced beef or lamb well spiced, using garlic, onions etc. Keep it rather dry, or the puffs will leak when baked. Add some chutney or sultanas. Roll out the pastry very thinly, and cut out fluted rounds with a 2 or 3 inch pastry cutter. Put a teaspoon of curry mixture on each. Brush one edge with beaten egg yolk and pinch together firmly. Brush top with egg and make a very small cut on the top. Bake about 10 minutes in a hot oven.

These can be frozen, unbaked and keep well. Bake from frozen and allow a little extra time.

Hermione Ball
Kent

Lemon Squash

4 lemons thinly sliced
1 oz tartaric acid
1 oz citric acid
2 lb sugar, granulated
1 oz Epsom salts

Put ingredients into a jug and pour on 2 pints of boiling water, stirring so that sugar dissolves. Leave covered in a cool place for 24 hours. Strain into bottles. Dilute about two tablespoons in a glass of water. In warm weather, store bottles in fridge.

Mrs Christopher Rowe
Sussex

Aunt Mary's Fudge

1 tin Nestlé full cream condensed milk
1½ cups water
2 tbsp golden syrup
2 lb caster sugar
4 oz butter
Vanilla to flavour

Put all in a large, heavy bottomed saucepan and bring to boil, stirring all the time. Boil hard for 10 minutes, until darkish golden colour and thick. Test in a cup of water and when sample feels hard, like toffee, take off and beat until a fudgy texture appears - (grainy!). Put into square shallow cake tin, maybe 2 tins if they are small - don't forget to grease them.

Edward Fox

Elderflower Cordial

23 elderflower heads, washed
3¼ tbsp granulated sugar
2 sliced lemons
2 oz citric acid
2½ pints boiling water

Make syrup, add lemons and acid. Cool and pour over elderflowers - leave for 24 hours. Strain and bottle. Freezes well.

Vivien Owston
Kent

Deep Fried "Seaweed"

(As served in Chinese restaurants, and as everyone knows is actually cabbage!)

About 450 g / 1 lb fresh spring greens
1 tbsp light Muscovado sugar
Oil for deep frying
½ tsp fine salt

You need to use the greenest leaves so you may need more than the quantity stated and keep the inner leaves for another meal! Wipe the leaves with damp kitchen paper to remove any grit but don't wash them or they will be too wet. Cut out the coarse central stems. Pile the leaves on top of one another, then roll the stack into a tight cylinder. Using a sharp knife, cut the roll into very, very thin slices. Then spread out and leave to dry for about an hour. Heat a deep pan of oil until very hot and cook a portion of the greens for 1 - 2 minutes. They should only be cooked till they are brilliant green: they will be soft but will crisp on drying. (Do not over cook to a greeny - brown.) Using a slotted spoon, remove from oil to drain on kitchen paper. Continue till all greens are cooked. Arrange in a heap on a serving dish seasoning lightly with salt. Sprinkle the raw sugar on top and then serve.

Libby Cox
London

Snowcapped Beetroot Mousse

Topping:

2 tsp gelatine
½ cup hot water
¾ cup mayonnaise
120 g cream cheese

Beetroot Mousse:

450 g jar or fresh cooked beetroot
3 tsp gelatine
½ cup hot water
1 tsp sugar
2 tbsp beetroot juice (or vinegar if using fresh beetroot)

Garnish:

Radishes
Parsley

Make the topping by dissolving the gelatine in the hot water and cooling slightly. Add the mayonnaise to cream cheese mixing until blended. Stir in the cooled gelatine and pour into prepared mould. Allow to set. Process the beetroot and place on top of the set topping. For the mousse, dissolve the gelatine in the hot water and beetroot juice (or vinegar), add the sugar and make up to 1½ cups with water. Season to taste with salt and pepper. Chill the mixture until just starting to set and then pour over the chopped beetroot in the mould and allow to set. Unmould onto a silver tray and garnish with radishes and parsley.

This is such a pretty salad, especially at Christmas time.

Mrs Alistair Gilson
Natal

Bacon and Onion Dumplings

1 lb short crust pastry
6 medium sized onions
6 oz bacon
Pepper and salt

Blanch the onions, cover with cold water and simmer for ten minutes. Strain the onions and cook in a slow oven until they are tender but unbroken (about 30 minutes). Take out the centres and chop them with the bacon. Add pepper and salt. Place mixture in centre of the onions. Roll out the pastry, cut it into six rounds and place an onion on each. Moisten the edges, draw up and press well together. Turn onto a greased shallow tin and bake in a hot oven (centre shelf) for about thirty minutes. These can be eaten hot with gravy or left to cool.

James Lewis
London

Curry Dip

1 large packet Philadelphia cheese
2 tsp Worcester Sauce
¼ - ½ tsp curry powder
3 dstsp cream
½ tsp salt

1. Cream cheese, gradually adding cream and Worcester Sauce.
2. Add curry powder and salt beating well.
3. Cover and leave overnight if possible for flavour to develop.
4. Put into serving bowl - serve with potato crisps or strips of carrot, cucumber and celery.

Mrs John Martin
Kent

Ming Sing

1 onion
3 tbsp long grain rice
½ an apple (chopped)
1 level tsp curry powder
Pepper
1 packet chicken noodle soup
1½ lb mince
½ cabbage (chopped)
1 oz sultanas
Pinch herbs
2 cups cold water
3 level tbsp tomato paste

Slice and fry onion, add mince and brown it. Add long-grain rice, tomato paste, cabbage, apple, sultanas, curry powder, pinch of herbs, pepper and cold water. Simmer for 30 minutes, then add packet of chicken noodle soup and cook a further 15 minutes.

Serve as an all-in-one meal with garlic bread.

Mrs S Lewers
Derbyshire

Roasted Tomatoes

Serves 6

Serve as starter, hot with Italian bread, cold with raised pies, flans and salads. Also ideal for BBQs.

12 medium sized tomatoes cored
3 cloves garlic chopped finely
1 oz parsley
Salt
2 heaped teaspoons sugar, granulated,
Olive oil
1 oz coriander
1 oz basil
Black pepper

Old slightly wrinkled tomatoes are ideal as they are full of flavour. The herbs should be finely chopped and fresh. When out of season, quantities may be reduced slightly and replaced by freeze dried.

1. Place cored tomatoes in baking dish, fill with chopped herbs, garlic and olive oil.
2. Sprinkle sugar over tomatoes and add salt and pepper.
3. Add one last fine drizzle of olive oil over tomatoes.
4. Cook for about 1 hour at 200°C. (The juice should be thick and rich and tomatoes very soft with roasted skins.)
5. Serve hot or leave to cool, sprinkle with a little of the remaining chopped herbs to garnish.

Wendy Simmons

Courgette Bake

1 lb courgettes
4 oz spring onions
Salt and pepper
4 tbsp fresh white breadcrumbs
1 tbsp fresh dill (very good with mint instead)
3 tbsp butter
1 tbsp chopped parsley
¼ pt soured cream or yoghurt

Grate the courgettes and bring to the boil in salted water. Drain. Melt one tablespoon butter and sauté chopped onions till soft. Stir in courgettes, fresh herbs, salt and pepper and cream or yoghurt. Pat into dish. Top with breadcrumbs and dot with butter. Bake for 30 minutes in moderate oven. Serve with meat or as a supper dish on its own.

Catherine McCully
Kent

Runner Bean Chutney (a favourite Devon recipe)

2 lb runner beans
1½ lb demerara sugar
1½ tbsp cornflour
1½ pints spiced vinegar
4 or 5 large onions
1½ tbsp mustard
1½ tbsp turmeric

Finely chop or mince beans and onions. Then boil in salted water until tender. Drain well. Add 1¼ pints of the vinegar to the beans and onions. Boil for 15 minutes. Mix cornflour, mustard and turmeric with half a pint of vinegar. Add demerara sugar and boil it for 15 minutes. Cool slightly and pot.

Pat Silvester
Devon

Quick Flaky Pastry

8 oz plain strong flour
Pinch salt
Plastic bag
6 oz marg (must be hard)
Cold water

Take fat hard from fridge. Wrap in foil and freeze for half an hour. Sift flour and salt into bowl. Hold marg in foil, dip into flour and grate on coarse grater placed over flour. Keep dipping marg into flour. With a palette knife, cut fat into flour until crumbly, (do not use your hands). Add enough water to make dough which leaves the sides of the bowl clean. Place dough in plastic bag and relax in fridge for half an hour.

Joanna Shepherdson
Kent

Sally O'Brien's Irresistible Cheesy Snacks

1 onion
4 tbsp mayonnaise
4 oz drained prawns
8 oz cream cheese
3 tbsp Parmesan

Get out your Magimix. Add these in order. One onion. Watch it whizz about and weep. Chuck in eight ounces of proper cream cheese! (Don't be such a meanie!) Add four tablespoons of mayonnaise. Okay you can use calorie - reduced if you insist, for me Hellmans always wins the day. Hurl in 3 large tablespoons of Parmesan.

Finally, add the vital mystery ingredient, which is four ounces of drained prawns, without which you will have dull, everyday, and deeply ordinaire cheesy things. Then refrigerate your mixture for half an hour.

Meanwhile (isn't there always a meanwhile?), using the smallest pastry cutter, cut rounds of sliced bread (you should have about four dozen) and toast these on one side. Spread your mixture on the toasted side. Pop them in a lowish oven for about 20 minutes until golden brown. Serve and abandon your diet.

Dillie Keane

Chocolate Sauce

4 dstsp milk
Mars bar

Get saucepan and put milk in. Heat this up as you slice thin slices off a Mars bar into it. Stir viciously with wooden spoon. Pour this delectable choc sauce onto ice cream.

Sir Ranulph Fiennes

Gratin Dauphinois

Serves 6

1.3 kg (3 lb) waxy potatoes
Salt and pepper
75 g (3 oz) butter
1 clove garlic
275 ml (½ pt) milk
Grated nutmeg (small amount)
275 ml (½ pt) double cream
150 g (5 oz) grated Gruyère cheese

Heat the oven to 160°C / 325°F / gas 3. Peel the potatoes, wipe clean with a damp cloth and slice them thinly. (Do not wash or soak them in water as this removes the starch which helps achieve the consistency.) Pour the milk into a large saucepan, season with salt, freshly ground pepper and nutmeg (just lightly cover the area of the milk with freshly ground pepper and some salt) and add the butter which has been cut into small pieces. Place over a medium heat, beat with a fork and bring slowly to boiling point. Add the potatoes and the cream gradually, reduce the heat and simmer very slowly for 10 minutes stirring frequently. Rub a large gratin dish with cut clove of garlic, butter it generously and pour in the potato mixture. Scatter the cheese on top and bake very slowly for 1½ hours until a brown crust has formed. Serve immediately.

Yvette d'Arcy
Middlesex

Ratatouille and Cashew Nut Bake

Serves 4

2 medium onions
1 small aubergine or 2 leeks
1 clove garlic
2 - 3 tbsp oil
3 small courgettes
1 green or red pepper (or ½ each)
1 tsp basil or oregano
400 g (14 oz) can tomatoes

Topping:

1 small onion studded with 2 cloves
25 g (1 oz) margarine
Seasoning
50 g (2 oz) cashew nut pieces
50 g (2 oz) grated cheese
1 bay leaf
25 g (1 oz) flour
250 ml (½ pt) milk
2 tbsp breadcrumbs

1. Put milk in pan with onion and cloves and bayleaf. Bring to boil slowly. Leave to stand.
2. Prepare vegetables - cut into even sized pieces.
3. Fry onions in oil, add peppers. Add other vegetables, herbs and seasoning. Cover, and simmer for 20 minutes until pulpy. Place in ovenproof dish.
4. Drain milk, discarding onion, cloves and bayleaf. Make béchamel sauce with milk, flour and margarine.
5. Add nuts and pour over ratatouille.
6. Top with breadcrumbs and grated cheese.
7. Brown under grill.

Jane Alvey
Sussex

Champ

Serves 4

1½ lb freshly cooked mashed potatoes
10 spring onions or 2 leeks, cooked in half cup of milk
4 tbsp melted butter   Salt and pepper

Cook the chopped spring onions, green part as well as white, in the milk. Drain and keep the milk. Mash the potatoes, season to taste and add the spring onions. Beat well together and add enough hot milk to make the dish creamy and smooth. Place the mixture in a deep, warmed dish, making a well in the centre and pour the hot melted butter into well. The dry potatoes should be dipped in the pool of butter when serving.

Champ can also be made with chopped parsley, chives, young nettle tops or young green peas. In the latter case, the peas are kept whole and added last. For a supper dish, scrambled eggs are often served in the centre and sprinkled with parsley.

My great grandmother was Irish and she has passed on to me a great love of the potato. This dish will not cost much to make in time or trouble - yet on a winter's night it will kindle the coldest heart.

Jeremy Irons

Cheese and Marmite Hot Tea Cake

90 g butter
1 beaten egg
1½ cups flour
Salt
¾ cup sugar
1 cup milk
2 tsp baking powder

Topping:

Marmite
1 cup grated cheese
½ cup melted butter

Cream the butter and sugar together, add egg and milk and mix well. Sift in dry ingredients. Bake in a pyrex dish or loose bottomed cake tin at 190°C for about 25 - 30 minutes. When baked spread with marmite and pour melted butter over cake. Sprinkle with cheese and serve hot.

Note: If you are not going to serve it immediately, keep cheese aside and only sprinkle over just before serving and after reheating.

Di McKenzie
Kent

Savoury Suet Dumpling Mix

4 oz SR flour
Pinch salt
Small amount chopped onion
2 oz shredded suet
Chopped herbs (sage, thyme etc)

Put all ingredients into a basin. Mix with a little cold water to form a stiff dough. Flatten into a round about one inch thick and fry in a little oil, turning once, or cook in a shallow tin with a little oil in the oven, until brown and crisp. May also be used in the conventional way, dividing into small amounts and adding to a stew for the last 15 minutes cooking.

Mrs Joan Wood
Kent

Somerset Herb Cheese

½ lb Cheddar cheese
2 tbsp chopped chives and parsley
6 tbsp cream

Grate the cheese and with the other ingredients render it down in a double saucepan, stirring all the time for maximum creaminess. Pour into small pots and cool. The herbs make it a delicate green-blue in colour.

Amanda Pope
Somerset

White Wine Sauce for Chicken or Fish

Fry portions of fish or chicken in butter till cooked. Remove from pan and keep warm. Pour half a glass of wine into pan and reduce to one tablespoon. Pour in half a glass of double cream, add snipped chives and / or parsley and salt and pepper. Warm gently and pour a little on beaten egg yolk, mix and return to pan. Warm through stirring carefully. Do not boil. Pour over fish or whatever.

Mrs Reg Older
Kent

Jo Kenney's Butterscotch Sauce

2 tbsp golden syrup
2 tbsp butter
2 tbsp double cream
3 tbsp brown sugar
Pinch salt

Put the syrup, sugar, butter and salt into a saucepan and bring slowly to nearly boiling point, stirring all the time. Remove from the heat and stir in the cream. This is particularly delicious with fresh peaches which have been peeled, cut into slices and served in a bowl of sugar syrup.

Mrs Richard Jenkins
Cambridgeshire

Quarante Quatre Digéstif

1 orange
44 sugar lumps
1 litre kilner jar
44 coffee beans
Calvados (about ¾ litre)

Make 44 slits in the orange and place in kilner jar with the rest of the ingredients. Leave for 44 days before sampling. Shake occasionally to dissolve sugar.

The longer you can bear to leave it the greater it tastes.

Mme Isobelle Acher
Cerisy - La - Forêt

Welsh Salad Dressing

2 egg yolks
1 tsp butter
4 tbsp vinegar
Salt and pepper
1 tsp sugar
1 tsp mustard
8 tbsp oil

Place the egg yolks in a basin and add the mustard, salt, pepper and sugar. Mix thoroughly to form a paste. Slowly add two tablespoons of vinegar and stir well. If there is any sign of curdling add a little flour. Add the oil, drop by drop and stir with a wooden spoon until the mixture is thick. Add the remaining vinegar slowly and beat well.
A richer, smoother dressing may be obtained by folding in one part whipped cream to every two parts mayonnaise.

James Lewis
London

Bean Salad

Excellent for buffets and BBQs

1 tin barlotti beans
1 tin kidney beans
1 red or green pepper, chopped
1 tin chick peas
1 tin green beans
1 red or white onion, chopped

Place all the above ingredients in a large mixing bowl.

Marinade / dressing:

½ cup vinegar
½ cup sugar
1 tsp mustard
½ tsp basil
½ cup oil
1 tsp salt
½ tsp tarragon
2 tbsp parsley

Marinade for at least 24 hours, stirring occasionally. Drain off some of the liquid prior to serving.

Henrietta Laitt
Kent

Hot Chilli Sauce

2 oz dried chillies
¼ bottle white vinegar
½ tsp salt
6 oz sugar
2 cloves garlic, chopped
1 tsp finely grated ginger

1. Put all ingredients in the pan and cook until chillies are soft.
2. Cool, then purée in the blender.
3. Pour in sterilised bottles and seal.

Keeps for months in the fridge. A few drops liven up baked potatoes and cheese, or use in curries, stir fries and baked beans.

Penny Hodson
Nottinghamshire

Chocolate Fudge

1½ cups brown sugar
½ cup milk
2 tbsp cocoa
1 tsp butter

Put all the ingredients except the butter in a saucepan and bring to the boil for 12 minutes. Add the butter and beat until thick. If it is cooked it should form a small ball if you drop some of the mixture into a cup of cold water.

Joanna 'Bunchy' Tollemache
London

Universal Goo

To serve as a separate sauce, or to mix with any cooked meats

2 medium onions (chopped)
½ large green pepper (chopped)
2 tbsp olive oil
¼ pt malt vinegar
2 tbsp grainy mustard
Scant tsp chilli sauce
Salt
1 tbsp flour mixed in a little water
½ lge red pepper (chopped)
4 sticks celery
½ pt stock or water
2 tbsp tomato purée
2 tbsp lemon juice
Good shaking ground black pepper
¼ tsp paprika

Having softened the vegetables in oil in a heavy saucepan, add everything else and simmer gently for approximately ½ - ¾ hour. The resulting "goo" will beautify a barbecue, liven up leftovers or even, at a pinch, delight a dinner party!

Anonymous

Saint Clement's Cordial

Juice of 8 oranges (1¼ pt)
Finely grated zest of 2 oranges
2 lb sugar
Juice of 6 lemons (12 fl oz)
Finely grated zest of 2 lemons

Put the juice and the grated zest into a saucepan. Add the sugar and stir over a low heat until the sugar has completely dissolved. Increase the heat and bring to just below boiling point. Remove from the heat immediately and leave to cool completely.

Line a plastic sieve with a double layer of muslin. Strain the pulp through it into a non-metallic bowl. Gather the corners of the muslin and lightly squeeze to extract all the juice possible. Pour into sterilised bottles to within an eighth of an inch of the tops. Seal the bottles, label and keep in the refrigerator. Makes about 2½ pints. Serve the cordial with an equal amount of either iced, still or sparkling water.

Mrs Vyvyan Harmsworth
Kent

Chapter 3

Fish

Whitstable Scallops in Creamy Sauce

A marinated shellfish dish flavoured with shallots and herbs.

Serves 6

12 scallops
½ bottle dry white wine
½ tablespoon chopped tarragon
½ tablespoon chopped chives
2 oz / 50 g unsalted butter
5 oz / 150 ml double cream
6 tablespoons fresh breadcrumbs
Sea salt
6 scallop shells
2 tablespoons chopped shallots
½ tablespoon chopped fennel
½ tablespoon chopped parsley
2 oz / 50 g plain flour
5 oz / 150 ml crème fraîche
3 tablespoons melted butter
White pepper

Take the scallops out of their shells and scrape off the beard-like fringe and intestinal thread. Cut away the orange flesh. Wash well and pat dry. Cut the scallops into three slices and the coral into two slices. Scrub the shells well and dry or use china scallop dishes. Chop up the shallot finely. Chop up the herbs finely and reserve one tablespoon of these for the sauce. Put the scallops in a bowl and add the wine, chopped shallots and remaining chopped herbs. Cover with cling film and leave to marinate for several hours in the fridge.

Transfer the scallops in their marinade to a saucepan and poach lightly for 5 minutes. Lift out the scallops onto a plate and reduce the wine by rapidly boiling for 5 minutes. Melt the butter in another saucepan, stir in the flour off the heat and add the strained marinade stirring well. Return to the heat and when the sauce is cooked through and lightly thickened add the cream and the crème fraîche and continue stirring for a few more minutes.

Add the scallops and the remaining chopped herbs. Season well with ground sea salt and ground pepper. Spoon into the scallop shells. Sprinkle the top of the scallops with the breadcrumbs and sprinkle with melted butter.

Heat the oven to gas 5 / 180°C. Cook the scallops for 20 minutes and serve with warm brown rolls.

Mrs Beverley Parker
Kent

Tuna Casserole

1 oz flour
½ pt milk
6 oz grated cheese
2 hard boiled eggs (sliced)
3 tomatoes
1 oz butter
Salt and pepper
7 oz tinned tuna
2 - 3 sticks celery

Make a cheese sauce - when roux has thickened add cheese and remove from heat. Drain oil / brine from tuna and break up fish with fork into a small casserole dish. Season fish with dash of Worcestershire sauce, dash Tabasco and garlic salt if desired. Place the sliced tomatoes on top of fish, followed by chopped celery and sliced hard boiled eggs. Completely cover with cheese sauce. Sprinkle with grated cheese and / or breadcrumbs and bake for 30 minutes in moderate oven, 350°F until golden brown.

Di Brown
Kent

Coquille Saint-Jacques les Rochers

Coquilles St Jacques 3 - 4 per person
Crème cru (or crème fraîche)
Salt and pepper
Butter for frying
White wine
Parsley to garnish

Slice coquilles in half if very large, otherwise leave whole. Melt butter in a saucepan and toss coquilles until gently cooked - about 4 minutes. Add a teaspoon of flour and work into butter, then slowly add white wine a little at a time until the sauce is creamy. Now add a large teaspoon of crème cru. Season with a little salt and a good sprinkling of ground pepper. Serve in individual dishes with a garnish of chopped parsley.

We have wonderful fresh coquilles in the markets in season, but one can buy bags of frozen, ready shelled ones in supermarkets, which are very good. Defrost before using them.

Mrs Peter Alliott
Normandy, France

Bacalao Al Ajoarriero (Cod with Garlic and Tomato)

In Spain there are many ways to prepare cod, as many ways as there are different regional cuisines. Being a long way from the North Atlantic waters, and long before freezing existed, traditionally the only way to get cod in Spain was in it's cured form (dried and salted). Due to this all recipes use dry salted cod as an ingredient. And of course the fish has to be desalted. Still, in Spain it is easier to find salted cod and the classic recipes are still used, though, if available, it may be easier and less time consuming to use fresh cod, thus saving the overnight process of desalting the fish. If you can get it, I recommend using salt cod. The taste is much better.

One of the more typical ways of preparing cod is the one called "Bacalao al ajoarriero," a very characteristic dish of Northern Spain. The ingredients in this recipe are all natural, making this dish not only a savoury but also a healthy one.

Our recipe has a little bit of a story. It was one of the favourite dishes of Ernest Hemingway. He tried this dish during the famous fiestas of San Fermin in Pamplona in 1926 in a little unpretentious restaurant called Casa Marceliano. The author said several times that one of his favourite dishes was this cod fixed in the Pamplona style. Casa Marceliano, a place full of tradition for the natives of Pamplona and almost mythical to those foreigners trapped in the spirit of this city and its fiesta, closed its doors after the Sanfermines of 1992. Unfortunately they won't serve any more bacalao al ajoarriero, but maybe we can try.

Serves 4

600 g desalted cod without spines
Olive oil
4 - 5 tomatoes
Oregano
6 medium cloves garlic
One large green pepper
Salt & pepper
200 g peeled shrimps

Put the salted cod in a bowl of cold water and let it stay set for approximately 20 hours, changing the water three times during this period. Once the cod is desalted (try it first and if still salty leave it for a longer time changing again the water) drain the water, remove the spines and cut it into small pieces (shredded). Set aside. Peel the tomatoes (a good trick is to put them for some minutes into boiling water). Squeeze the peeled tomatoes to drain the water and seeds and cut them into small pieces. Cut the green pepper in small pieces and chop the garlic finely. Cover the bottom of a clay pot of 25 - 30 cm in diameter with olive oil and when hot add the pepper and the garlic. Fry them till the garlic turns golden and then add the chopped tomatoes. Simmer on a low flame, stirring it occasionally till you have a soft, almost liquid mixture. Add the cod and mix it with the tomato paste. Then let it simmer for five minutes without stirring. Taste it and add salt and pepper if needed. Add the peeled shrimp and let it simmer for 5 to 10 minutes more.

Serve it in the same clay pot, accompanied by a mixed salad of lettuce, tomato, onion, cucumber, peeled and roasted red pepper, black olives dressed with olive oil, wine vinegar and salt. Accompany it with a rosé wine (vino rosado) from Navarra if possible.

Bon appetit!

Dr Ana Cerón
Spain

Salmon, Bacon and Herbs en Papillotte

Serves 4

4 salmon steaks
4 sprigs rosemary
Salt and pepper
4 bits of back bacon
Butter

Sauté the salmon in butter for about two minutes on each side. Put a large bit of foil in a baking tin and brush it with a bit of melted butter and put the fish on it then a bit of bacon on top, then the rosemary and salt and pepper and pour over the remainder of the melted butter you cooked the fish in. Then make the foil like a parcel, scrunch it up so its airtight, cover the top and shove it in the top oven of the Aga for 15 minutes, 450°F. Its delicious and keeps it all moist and juicy. Serve with lemon, of course.

Fiona Gault
Kent

Quick Fish with Quick Sauce

Butter an ovenproof dish and put in as many pieces of cod or haddock as required - not overlapping. On top sprinkle a mixture of breadcrumbs and grated cheese. Dot with butter and put in oven at 170°C until fish is cooked and topping crunchy. Serve with sauce made from mayonnaise with capers and chopped parsley mixed in.

Mrs Christopher Garfit
Dorset

Morton's Fresh Salmon Fishcakes

1 lb salmon tail
1 bay leaf
6 peppercorns
1½ lb floury potatoes
1 tbsp double cream
Little flour
2 oz fine white breadcrumbs, toasted
1 lemon
Seasoning
1 small glass dry white wine
1 oz butter
1 level tsp paprika
1 egg, beaten

For frying:

1 oz clarified butter (see instructions)
1 tbsp vegetable oil

Sauce:

Reduced fish stock
2 tbsp double cream
1 heaped tbsp capers plus juice

Lay the salmon tail in a baking dish, squeeze over the juice of half the lemon, sprinkle on a little salt, add the bay leaf and peppercorns and pour over the white wine and equal amount of water. Cover with tin foil and bake at 170°C / 325°F / gas 3 for 25 minutes and allow to cool in it's juices. Remove the skin and bones from the salmon. Tip the juices into a pan and bubble this stock for 5 minutes and strain into a bowl to use later with the caper sauce. Peel, cook and mash the potatoes, adding the butter, double cream and plenty of seasoning including the paprika. Flake the salmon into a bowl, squeeze over the juice of the remaining half lemon, fold in the mashed potato and check for seasoning. Make into 8 fishcakes, shape, dust with flour, paint with lightly beaten egg and cover with toasted breadcrumbs.

To clarify butter:

Melt gently in a saucepan and drain the clear butter from the white impurities that settle on the bottom of the pan. Combine the clarified butter and frying oil in a pan and fry the fishcakes until golden on both sides. Keep warm in the oven until required.

To make the sauce:

Heat the stock and capers plus a little caper juice, stir in cream, bubble momentarily and serve with the fishcakes on a bed of lightly garlicked spinach.

Julian Jeffery
Morton's, Berkeley Square

Salmon Mornay

2 oz butter
Salt and pepper
Pinch cayenne pepper
3 gherkins
7 oz can salmon
4 spring onions
1 tbsp plain flour
¼ tsp dry mustard
2½ cups milk
2 hard boiled eggs
1 chicken stock cube

Topping:

1 cup fresh breadcrumbs
1 oz cheese, grated
1 tbsp chopped parsley
2 tbsp butter, melted

1. Melt butter. Add flour, salt and pepper, mustard and cayenne pepper. Cook stirring for 1 minute.
2. Gradually add milk. Stir until sauce thickens. Cook for one minute.
3. Remove from heat and add finely sliced gherkins, roughly chopped eggs, salmon (drained and flaked), crumbled stock cube & chopped spring onions.
4. Put in greased ovenproof dish.
5. Make the topping by combining the melted butter with other ingredients and sprinkle over salmon mixture.
6. Bake in a moderate oven,180°C for 20 - 25 minutes till heated through.

Mrs Glen Meyer
New Zealand

Trout in White Wine and Grapes

Serves 4

Cooking time: 30 to 40 minutes

It was the Romans who first planted vines in southern England and made wine from the grapes. For some centuries after their departure from these shores, wine-making in this country was neglected. Today it has been revived and the vineyards are beginning to thrive. Experts from other wine-producing countries acknowledge the fact that the best of English wines are of high quality and worthy of attention. Many classic British recipes include wine to add flavour and, in some cases, to help tenderize the meat. Most fish is very soft and tender but sometimes river-caught trout are large and not as succulent as smaller fish, or those that are farm-produced, and the wine helps to rectify this.

4 trout
Freshly ground black pepper, to taste
Pinch ground cinnamon
50 g (2 oz) butter
300 ml (½ pt) dry white wine
1 fresh bay leaf or ½ dried bay leaf
Salt, to taste
1 level tbsp plain flour
About 100 g (4 oz) grapes, preferably half black and half white

Clean the trout and remove the heads. Place in a casserole with the wine, a little seasoning, the bay leaf and ground cinnamon. If the trout are large and old, allow the fish to marinate in the wine for an hour. If they are small and young then leave for 10 minutes only, otherwise the fish will become over-soft. Preheat the oven to 190°C / 375°F / gas 5. Cover the dish and bake the fish. Small trout will take about 25 minutes but older ones need about 35 minutes. Do not over-cook the fish, for it must remain firm for frying after baking. Deseed the grapes, they need not be skinned for this dish. Lift the fish from the liquid and drain well, then dry on absorbent paper. Heat the butter in a large frying pan and add the fish. Turn in the butter and fry until the skin turns golden in colour. Remove from the pan to a heated dish. Stir the flour into the butter remaining in the pan, then strain the wine used in baking into this. Stir over a low heat until slightly thickened. If much of the wine has evaporated during cooking you will need a little more. Add the grapes and heat for a short time. Spoon the sauce and grapes around the trout.

Marguerite Patten from her book 'Classic British Dishes'

Cod in a Cheese and Bacon Crust

Per person:

7 oz fillet cod
2 rashers unsmoked bacon, diced
Knob butter
2 oz Cheddar, grated
2 oz fresh breadcrumbs
Salt and pepper

For the herb sauce:

2 oz butter
2 tsp chopped mixed fresh herbs

To serve:

Wedges of lemon

Preheat oven to gas 6. Butter a shallow gratin dish. Place the fish in the dish and season with salt and pepper. Mix the cheese, bacon and breadcrumbs together, sprinkle over the fish and dot the top with butter. Bake the fish for 10 - 15 minutes, or until cooked. Gently melt the butter, stir in the herbs and pour round the fish. Serve with wedges of lemon.

Mrs Richard Jenkins
Cambridgeshire

Fish Cakes

8 oz crabmeat, raw salmon and cod
Zest of lime
1 tbsp chopped coriander leaves
5 oz boiled spuds
1 tbsp lime juice
2 spring onions chopped and green bits
Capers (optional)

Peel & grate potatoes, then lightly boil for 10 minutes. Boil more and mash if in a hurry. Put them in a bowl with the fish and mix gently. Add cayenne pepper and salt to taste. Make into eight fish cakes. Leave for two hours and fry in hot oil, three minutes each side.

Vivien Owston
Kent

Coquilles Saint-Jacques de Normandie

This is not my recipe but one given to me in the market at St. Lô, and has been much enjoyed. I merely translate it!

4 or 5 coquilles (St Jacques) per person according to size
1 soup spoon olive oil
1 soup spoon crème fraîche
4 spices seasoning
1 soup spoon Noilly
Cayenne pepper

Marinate the coquilles in their shells for 1 hour with olive oil, cayenne pepper and "4 spices" seasoning. In a non-stick saucepan, quickly cook the coquilles. Remove, set aside and keep warm. Add Noilly to pan juices then the crème fraîche. Allow to cook gently until sauce thickens and coats back of spoon.

Serve hot, possibly accompanied with a little spinach or rice.

Mrs Peter Alliott
Normandy, France

Roast Salmon With A Peanut Crust

Serves 4

1 red chilli
175 g (6 oz) unsalted butter, softened
Finely grated rind of 1 lime
75 g (3 oz) salted roasted peanuts
2.5 cm (1 in) piece fresh root ginger
3 level tbsp chopped fresh parsley
3 - 4 spring onions
125 g (4 oz) fresh white breadcrumbs
Salt and pepper
4 salmon fillets, about 175 g (6 oz) each (skinned if wished)

1. Finely chop the chilli. Peel and grate the root ginger. Beat these into the unsalted butter with the fresh parsley and lime rind. Finely chop the spring onions and roughly process the peanuts in a liquidiser.
2. Fry the breadcrumbs with the spring onions and peanuts in 50 g (2 oz) of the flavoured butter until golden, stirring continuously to prevent the breadcrumbs from sticking together. Season.
3. Arrange the salmon fillets, skin side uppermost, in a roasting tin. Spoon the fried breadcrumb mixture on the top. Cook at 200°C / 400°F / mark 6 for 10 - 15 minutes or until the salmon is just cooked.

4. Melt the remaining flavoured butter and serve with the roast salmon and boiled jacket potatoes.

If you are entertaining, serve a simple starter of roasted garlic tomatoes. Halve 6 tomatoes and arrange them, cut side uppermost, in a roasting tin. Season with salt, pepper and crushed garlic, to taste. Drizzle with olive oil and cook at 200°C / 400°F / mark 6 for 10 - 12 minutes or until softened. Serve the garlic tomatoes warm on a bed of mixed salad leaves.

Cook's Tip:

To save cooking time, make up a batch of the spicy flavoured butter and the fried peanut and breadcrumb topping and freeze ahead. Both of these mixtures can be used direct from the freezer; just allow an extra 2 - 3 minutes cooking time at step 3.

Moyra Fraser
Cookery Editor
Good Housekeeping Magazine

General Grudger

In a well greased shallow pie dish put a thin layer of mashed potatoes. Cover with grated cheese and mango chutney. Now another layer of mashed potatoes, just enough to cover. Next put a layer of any well flavoured fish - cooked (prawns are wonderful). Sprinkle with grated cheese and cover with slices of hard boiled egg. One more layer of potato. On top circle with rings of tomato and fill the space in the middle with the following:

1 tablespoon sultanas, previously soaked in a little milk
4 tablespoons browned breadcrumbs
1 tablespoon chopped parsley
1 dessertspoon curry powder (or more if you like it hot)

Bind all together with a little milk. Put a few knobs of butter on top and bake in a medium oven till hot through. Sprinkle with parsley before serving.

Mrs Susan Milton
Aberdeen

Salmon and Horseradish Coulibiac

Serves 6 - 8

Rough puff pastry:

225 g (8 oz) strong white flour
8 tablespoons iced water
175 g (6 oz) cold hard butter, diced
Egg yolk and milk to glaze

Filling:

1 bunch of spring onions, sliced
Large carton of crème fraîche
Salt and pepper
1½ - 2 tbsp creamed horseradish
700 - 800 g (1½ - 1¾ lb) salmon fillet, skinned and cubed
227 g can ready cooked wholegrain rice

First make the pastry:

Place the flour in a bowl, add the butter and toss round to coat it with flour. Using a flat bladed knife stir in the water to bind. Turn onto a lightly floured surface and form into a square. Roll out to a long thin rectangle, brush off any surplus flour and fold down the top 1/3 of the pastry. Brush off any flour and fold up the bottom 1/3 to make a neat package. press the edges together and turn once clockwise so the fold is on the right. Roll out and repeat the brushing and folding. Roll out a third time, brush and fold. Wrap and chill for at least 20 minutes. Roll and fold 3 more times, wrap and chill till ready to use.

To make the coulibiac:

Roll out the pastry to a 38 cm (15 inch) square and place it diagonally on a baking sheet. Cover with the rice and spring onions in a square. Season well. Arrange the salmon cubes on top. Mix the crème fraîche with horseradish to taste, season and spoon about 4 tablespoons over the salmon. Damp the pastry edges and fold up to make an envelope, pressing the edges together and trimming neatly. Cover and refrigerate until ready to cook.

Heat the oven to 210°C / 425°F / gas 7. Uncover the coulibiac and brush with egg or milk glaze and bake for 40 - 45 minutes. Serve with hollowed out tomatoes baked and filled with the remaining horseradish cream.

Mrs Peter Foster

Stuffed Plaice

Serves 6

6 large plaice fillets, black skin removed
300 ml (½ pt) fish or vegetable stock
75 g (3 oz) smoked cod's roe
50 g (2 oz) wholemeal breadcrumbs
150 ml (¼ pt) strained natural yoghurt
Freshly ground black pepper
Juice of 1 lemon

Have ready an ovenproof dish large enough to take the fillets folded in half and kept flat. Wash the fish and leave to drain. Skin the cod's roe and place in a food processor or liquidiser. Add the breadcrumbs, lemon juice, yoghurt and pepper and blend until smooth. Place the fish flat on a work surface and spread even amounts over one half of each fillet. Fold the other half over the top and transfer to the prepared dish. Pour over the stock and bake in the oven for 25 minutes, basting occasionally.

Stuffing the plaice with a homemade taramasalata mixture makes it a very special meal. If you like, you could add a tablespoon of concentrated tomato purée to the cod's roe mixture for more colour and flavour. Serve with new potatoes or brown rice and a green vegetable. The taramasalata may also be used on its own as a dip or spread.

Mrs Judith Fawcett
Hertford

Salmon in a Dishwasher!

Wrap salmon whole or in steaks tightly in tin foil. If whole, wrap head and tail in wet greaseproof or kitchen roll. Make sure it is totally sealed. Place in top of dishwasher. Do not add detergent. Put onto normal cycle. Leave. Will be cooked when finished. Unwrap, dress, serve.

Best done when salt level in dishwasher is low.

Sally Everist
London

Trout with Walnut and Horseradish Sauce

Serves 4

4 or 5 small trout or 1 large trout
Court bouillon for poaching

Court bouillon:

2 wineglasses good white wine
1 carrot, sliced
Salt and pepper
1 bouquet garni
1 onion, sliced

Wash and dry trout (if desired, de-bone leaving the head and tail on). The latter applies only to those with a delicate touch with fish. Care must be taken not to bruise or mutilate any fish when handling. Make the court bouillon and gently poach the trout for 10 - 15 minutes depending on size. DO NOT BOIL. Leave to cool and remove skin. Bones can also be removed at this stage.

Sauce:

60 g shelled and skinned walnuts
1 tsp sugar
Juice ½ lemon
2 tbsp freshly, finely grated horseradish
A little salt
125 ml thick cream

To skin walnuts, pour boiling water over them and rub off skins as soon as cool enough to handle. It is a tedious operation but well worth the effort. Chop finely. Stir lightly into cream and add the horseradish. Add the seasonings, and lastly the lemon juice.

Note: This sauce is also a good accompaniment to hot or smoked trout.

Glyn Hurt
S Africa

Fisherman's Wife's Chowder

I am married to an all-too-successful fisherman who keeps us over-supplied with trout and salmon all summer! I devised this recipe as a way of using cooked left-over fish when we have had enough of it with mayonnaise or in kedgeree, delicious though both are. You can make it as a soup or as a stew, and the quantity of the ingredients can be varied to taste. It is very versatile.

My fisherman thinks it is delicious!

Potatoes, scrubbed or peeled, and sliced thickly
Leeks washed and sliced into inch rings
A generous amount of butter - no substitutes
Milk
Cream
Cooked fish

Pour boiling water over the potatoes and leave while you prepare the leeks. Drain and shake the potatoes and put into a saucepan or casserole with the leeks, and plenty of butter. Shake the vegetables around in the butter. Add milk and cream in whatever proportions you wish, and cook over low heat or in a moderately hot oven for one hour. Remove from heat and immediately add flaked cooked fish, a pinch or two of salt, and plenty of freshly ground pepper. Serve at once, either as a dish on its own, or with chunks of fresh (preferably home-made) wholewheat bread.

Note - fish heads boiled up with or without a handful of thyme make delicious stock. You can use it with cream instead of milk.

Claire Peppiat
London

Haddock Monte Carlo

1½ Ib smoked haddock
1 oz butter
¼ pt milk
2 - 3 oz grated Gruyère cheese
½ Ib tomatoes
1 oz flour
¼ pt cream
Pepper and mace

Butter a shallow dish and lay skinned haddock fillets in one layer. Skin and slice tomatoes, cover fish, season with pepper only. Make the white sauce and season with pepper and mace and pour over fish and the tomatoes - sprinkle with the grated cheese. Put in top of oven for approximately 20 minutes or so. Brown under the grill.

Sue Webster
London

Sweetcorn Chowder with Prawns and Red Peppers

Serves 6

1 lb uncooked prawns, peeled and de-veined
1 large onion, peeled and finely chopped
2 medium red peppers, deseeded and thinly sliced
12 oz sweetcorn, tinned or frozen
Sprigs of parsley or fresh oregano / marjoram to garnish

2 tbsp olive oil	¾ pt milk
1 bay leaf	½ tsp dried marjoram or oregano
Pinch nutmeg	¾ pt chicken or fish stock
¼ pt single cream	12 oz potatoes, peeled and diced

1. Heat the oil in a large saucepan and soften the onion without browning.
2. Stir in the pepper, potatoes, sweetcorn, bay leaf, marjoram or oregano and nutmeg. Pour in the stock and bring to the boil. Reduce the heat and simmer for 10 - 15 minutes, until the potatoes are cooked.
3. Pour in the milk, season with black pepper. Bring back to the boil and add the prawns. Cook for 3 - 5 minutes until prawns are pink and cooked through.
4. Remove the bay leaf, stir in the cream. Heat through for 2 - 3 minutes without boiling.
5. Garnish and serve.

Laura Baxter

Fish Stew

Fry sliced potatoes in olive oil, then onion rings. Put both into casserole. Dust portions of fish with seasoned flour and add to the casserole, then cover with either fresh tomato sauce or tinned chopped tomatoes. Then cover with breadcrumbs. Bake for forty minutes. At half time add a little white wine.

Mrs Reg Older
Kent

Chapter 4

Main Courses

Meat

Crumbed Chops

6 pork chops
Egg
A few tomatoes, mushrooms and onion
Flour
1 packet sage and onion stuffing mix

Flour, egg and coat chops in dry stuffing mix. Press down hard. Fry the chops gently in hot fat. Chop tomatoes, mushrooms and onion and sauté gently. Put mixture in a shallow dish and lay chops on top. Cover in foil and cook in medium to hot oven for approximately 20 minutes. Take foil off and crisp up the mixture.

Mrs Richard Henderson
Kent

Elizabethan Pork

Serves 10

2 onions
Head of celery
6 oz seedless raisins
1 orange
2 large Cox's apples
1 oz plain white flour
Black pepper
3 cloves garlic, crushed
½ bottle red wine or cider or strong ale
1 level tsp of marjoram, thyme, cinnamon, mace,
3 lb leg of pork
8 oz tin apricots
1 lemon
6 oz stoned dates
1 tbsp clover honey
4 tbsp oil
Mild curry powder
Salt

NB: Boned and rolled hand of pork or shoulder is also satisfactory.

Trim the meat of any skin, bone and excess fat. Cut into half inch cubes and dredge in the seasoned flour. Heat some of the oil and fry the meat until lightly brown; this is best done a little at a time, transferring the fried cubes with a draining spoon to an ovenproof casserole. Next fry the finely sliced onions and celery, transferring them to the casserole. Then sprinkle over any remaining flour. Add the apricots, drained and roughly chopped, raisins (not sultanas), the juice and finely grated rind of the lemon and orange, the chopped dates and apples, honey, wine, herbs and spices etc. Cook for 2 hours at 350°F or until tender. Adjust seasoning and thickening if necessary. This recipe will freeze. Allow plenty of time to make, as preparing the pork and putting all the ingredients together takes longer than one expects.

Diana Hawkins
Kent

Festive Tourte

Makes 2 x 10" flans, each serving 6 - 8 people

8 oz marg
1 lb 4 oz plain flour
1 lb onions, finely chopped
8 oz fresh white breadcrumbs
Salt and pepper
2 lb minced pork
8 oz streaky bacon, trimmed
Baking beans
2 oz lard
2 level tsp salt
2 oz butter or marg
2 level tbsp dried parsley
2 large eggs, beaten
12 oz cheese, grated
14 oz pkt frozen puff pastry, thawed

Oven 375°F / 190°C / gas 5, shelves centre towards top

Sift flour and salt and rub in marg and lard to breadcrumb stage. Add sufficient water to bind together then knead lightly. Roll pastry out on a lightly floured surface and use to line two loose based 25 cm (10") flan tins 1¼" deep, (or flan ring and baking sheet). Prick bases, then line with greaseproof paper and baking beans. Bake for 15 minutes, then remove beans, cook 5 minutes. Gently fry onions until just soft, then combine with breadcrumbs, parsley, salt and pepper and nearly all the beaten egg. Remove flan cases from oven. Increase heat to 450°F / 230°C / gas 8. Season pork well with salt and pepper, then spread half in each of the flan cases and cover with cheese. Top with rashers of bacon. Halve the puff pastry, roll out each piece to a round to fit the top of a flan. Lightly fold each round in half and cut lines at half inch intervals almost across the pastry to the edge. Carefully lift and unfold cut tops on to the flans, sealing edges with beaten egg. Brush tops with beaten egg. Bake for 20 minutes, change shelf positions after 10 minutes, then reduce oven to 325°F / 170°C / gas 3 and cook a further 40 - 45 minutes. Serve cold.

Joanna Shepherdson
Kent

Pork à la Creme

Serves 4

4 lean slices of pork (fillet if possible)
Poupon Dijon mustard
2 medium onions
½ lb button mushrooms
½ pt (10 fl oz) cream

Gently sauté onions in oil and add pork, liberally smeared with mustard. Seal meat both sides. Season then reduce heat to minimum and cook covered until meat is tender. Add finely chopped mushrooms. Once cooked add cream and serve.

Mrs D Piper
Kent

Pork Casseroled with Fruit

½ oz butter
4 pork cutlets
8 oz pineapple rings
1 oz brown sugar
¼ pt single cream
1 tsp oil
14½ oz tin apricot halves
8 prunes stoned and chopped
5 tbsp chicken stock
Salt and pepper

Melt butter with oil in a frying pan. Add chops and brown on both sides. Remove from pan and drain and arrange in casserole. Drain apricot halves and pineapple rings, reserving syrup. Place fruit with prunes on top of chops to cover them. Sprinkle with brown sugar. Mix stock with five tablespoons each of apricot and pineapple syrups. Pour into casserole. Cover tightly and cook at 180°C for about 1 hour. Transfer chops to warmed serving dish keeping fruit in place. Boil liquid until reduced to a quarter of a pint. Skim off fat, stir in cream (or add a teaspoon of cornflour) and salt and pepper. Heat and pour over pork.

Mrs Dickie Chesters
Kent

Gin and Pork Chops

4 pork chops (thick with fat and rind)
2 oz dry vermouth
2 tbsp olive oil
2 oz gin
Lemon juice (½ lemon)
10 cloves garlic

Thyme and bay leaf
Capers
Salt and pepper

Place chops in shallow dish. Cut one clove of garlic into slivers and put into chops near the bone. Sprinkle with juice from half a lemon, gin and vermouth. Add crumbled bay leaf, pinch of thyme, season. Spoon over two tablespoons of olive oil. Marinade for at least 2 hours turning at will. Throw most of garlic into boiling water for 2 minutes. Drain, cool and peel. Chop roughly. Remove chops from marinade and pat dry. Melt butter and brown chops on both sides on high heat. Lower heat and add garlic. Cover dish and cook on low heat for half an hour, turning once. Remove chops when tender and keep warm. Add the marinade to the pan. Bubble, add two tablespoons of capers. Pour over chops - garnish with parsley.

Jennifer Dean
Kent

Thai Pork

Serves 4 - 6

1½ lb cubed pork (loin or shoulder)
2 garlic cloves
1 inch piece of root ginger
1½ tsp ground coriander
2 tbsp vegetable oil
1½ pt chicken stock
1 medium onion
1 medium lemon grass stalk
2 small hot chillies
Grated rind and juice of 1 lemon
Small tin chopped tomatoes
4 tbsp coconut milk powder

Peel garlic cloves. Peel and chop onion roughly. Halve and roughly chop lemon grass. Peel ginger, chop roughly. Halve and de-seed chillies. Put all, with the lemon rind and juice, into a liquidiser and process to a pulp - I use a coffee grinder. Cut the pork into bite size pieces. Heat oil in a large frying pan or casserole. Add paste and cook for three to four minutes stirring. Add pork and continue cooking and stirring for 5 minutes. Add chopped tomatoes and stock and the coconut milk powder, and bring to a boil. Simmer gently until cooked - this should take about half an hour. Serve accompanied with rice.

Caroline Lindley
London

Pork Chops

4 pork chops
Coarse grain mustard
Paprika
Flour
Tin of chopped tomatoes
Salt, pepper, etc

Coat the chops with the flour, and fry in some olive oil. Then add 2 - 3 dessertspoons of mustard along with the tin of tomatoes. Mix it all up. Add in a teaspoon of paprika, salt etc along with whatever herbs take your fancy - I like basil and oregano. Cover and leave, turning chops occasionally for 15 - 20 minutes and then serve.

NB This one is my own invention, inspired by the bare cupboards of a student house!

Patch Wilkinson
Southampton University

Pork Chops in Mustard

4 pork chops
3 tbsp stock or water
Salt and pepper
1 tbsp french mustard
1 oz / 25 g butter
¼ pt / 150 ml single cream
1 tbsp wine vinegar or orange juice

Rub chops with seasoning and fry in butter until they are browned on both sides and cooked through. Transfer to serving dish and keep warm. Stir vinegar and stock into pan juices, bring to the boil and simmer to reduce slightly. Remove from heat and stir in mustard followed by the cream. Pour over the chops and serve.

Mrs Peter Stevens
Kent

Pork Dish (can be done with chicken breasts)

2 - 3 pork fillets
4 oz mushrooms
1 glass sherry
Cream
2 onions
1 dstsp paprika
¼ pt stock
1 dstsp flour

Chop onion, cut fillet into pieces. Sauté, add paprika and cook for 2 - 3 minutes. Stir in one dessertspoon flour, add sherry and stock and bring to boil. Simmer gently for 30 - 40 minutes. Add mushrooms. Pour in cream and season, serve with rice or potatoes

Sue Webster
London

Provençale Veal

Serves 4 - 6

2 cloves garlic chopped
Olive oil
1 sprig rosemary, chopped
2 lb tomatoes, peeled, de-seeded and chopped
3 oz good quality black olives, stoned
2 lb shoulder of veal, cubed
Salt and pepper

Fry the garlic and veal in the oil until the meat is well browned. Add the tomatoes, a little salt and lots of black pepper. Cover and simmer for 1½ hours over a low heat. The sauce should be thick, but if it looks a little dry, add water. 10 minutes before serving, sprinkle with rosemary and stir in the olives.

Lunch or supper dish served with rice.

Mrs Jenny Ursell
Kent

Veal Escalopes

Veal escalopes
Eggs, beaten and seasoned
Salt and pepper
Anchovy paté (the tube variety)
Breadcrumbs

With a meat tenderiser, gently flatten the meat to almost twice its size and cut into approximately 3 - 4 inch squares. (One escalope will divide into 3 pieces. Two pieces are sufficient for 1 person.) Spread anchovy paté liberally on each piece before dipping in egg wash and breadcrumbs. Quickly fry in butter and a little oil, about 1 - 1½ minutes on each side. Serve immediately.

Mrs Peter Alliott
Normandy

Irish Stew with Dumplings

Serves 4

2½ lb lean middle neck and scrag of mutton or lamb
12 oz onions, sliced
4 oz mushrooms, sliced
1 large potato, peeled and sliced
2 tbsp seasoned flour
8 oz carrots, sliced
2 medium leeks, washed and sliced
2 pt chicken stock
Salt and pepper

For the dumplings:

4 oz self-raising flour
Pinch salt
2 oz shredded suet
Cold water to mix

Wipe pieces of meat and cut away any excess fat, then dip them in the seasoned flour. Place layers of meat in the bottom of a large saucepan, followed by some onion, carrot, mushrooms, leek and potato and season with salt and pepper. Then put in more meat and continue layering the ingredients until everything is in. Add approximately 2 pints of chicken stock and bring to simmering point. Spoon off any scum that appears on the surface, then cover the pan with lid and leave to simmer over a low heat for about 2 hours. About 15 minutes before the end of the cooking time, make the dumplings. Mix the flour, salt and suet and add sufficient cold water to make a fairly stiff but elastic dough that leaves the bowl cleanly. Divide the dough into eight pieces and roll each portion into a dumpling shape. When the stew is ready, remove the meat and vegetables onto a large warm serving dish. Cover with foil and keep warm. Season the liquid to taste and bring to the boil. Put the dumplings in, cover and cook for 20 - 25 minutes making sure they don't come off the boil. Serve the meat surrounded by the vegetables and dumplings with some of the liquid poured over and some in a gravy boat.

Mary Scanlon
Sligo, Ireland

Lamb Cutlets in Orange and Ginger

Lamb cutlets (one each or slices of leg of lamb)
Preserved ginger (approx half a piece per person)
Parsley or watercress for decoration

Flour seasoned with salt and pepper
Carton orange juice
Oil
Slices of orange for decoration

1. Trim the cutlets of all fat and dry on kitchen paper then coat with seasoned flour.
2. Heat thin layer of oil in frying pan and seal each cutlet but do not overcook. Meat is ready when blood starts to show through. Drain off excess oil and put in casserole dish.
3. Chop the ginger very finely and add in between layers of cutlets.
4. Cover with orange juice.
5. Put lid on casserole and put in oven at 225°F / 110°C / gas 4.
6. Cook 2 hours then remove lid set oven to 400°F / 200°C / gas 6 for 20 mins.
7. Serve with fried orange circles and parsley.
8. Jacket or mashed potatoes or chunks of fresh bread go well with this dish.

Lesley Lee

Herbed Rack of Lamb

1 prepared best - end of lamb
4 - 6 tbsp brown / white breadcrumbs
½ clove crushed garlic
1 egg yolk
1 bunch watercress to garnish
2 - 3 tbsp fresh chopped herbs, (parsley, rosemary, thyme)
2 tbsp walnut or olive oil
1 oz chopped walnuts
Grated lemon rind and juice
Salt, pepper and mace

Have the best-end chined, the back bone removed and bones exposed. Remove excess fat and lightly cut criss-cross lines in the fat. Spread with the herb mixture and pat on lightly. Wrap the tips of the bones in tinfoil. Roast the lamb in a hot oven for 25 - 30 minutes, depending on size, covering the top lightly with tin foil if the herb mixture gets too brown. Garnish with watercress and serve cut into cutlets.

Herb mixture:

Mix the chopped herbs, breadcrumbs and walnuts with the oil, crushed garlic, seasoning and egg yolk to make a firm paste.

Mrs Peter Stevens
Kent

Lamb in White Coffee

Trim excess fat from a leg of lamb (Aussie of course!!). Stud lamb with garlic cloves. Make strong white coffee. Place lamb in half a cup of coffee in a baking dish and bake in slow oven, 180°C for 15 minutes per lb (this is debatable - if you like pink lamb, watch it), basting frequently with coffee. When cooked to desired colour, remove. Over hot plate reduce coffee by a third, add 2 tablespoons of redcurrant jelly and when melted, 4 tablespoons of cream. Serve with green beans, mashed potato and additional redcurrant jelly. This is a delicate dish so it should not be overpowered by vegetables, but a good red wine is great. Good luck!

Mrs Judith James
Melbourne, Australia

Somerset Lamb Casserole

Serves 4 - 6

1 tsp corn oil
1 large onion - sliced
1 lb cooking apples, peeled and sliced
1½ - 2 lb middle neck lamb chops
1 lb potatoes - peeled and sliced
1 beef stock cube + 3 pint water

Heat corn oil in a pan, add the meat and onions and brown lightly. Cover sliced potatoes with cold water, add half a teaspoon of salt and bring to the boil. Drain the water off and arrange half the potato in a layer in the base of the casserole. Layer the meat, onion and sliced apple on top and finish with the remaining potato, brushed over with a little oil. Dissolve beef stock cube in water and pour into the casserole. Serve garnished with a little chopped parsley. Cook, uncovered, in a moderately hot oven 375°F / gas 5 for 1½ - 2 hours.

Amanda Pope
Somerset

Canadian Pam's Lamb and Rice

Serves 3

2 cups cooked lamb
4 tomatoes (peeled), or use tin
Season highly with salt & pepper
2 cups meat stock
2 onions (chopped small)

Combine above and cook gently for 15 minutes. Melt 3 tablespoons butter in pan. Stir in a quarter to half cup raw rice and cook until brown. Add 2 tablespoons Worcestershire sauce. Combine the rice and lamb. Bake 35 - 40 minutes in moderate oven. Excellent for left over lamb roast.

Mrs Stephen Saunders
Kent

Lamb Cutlets in Peppercorn Sauce

Cook lamb cutlets or fillets to your liking, then cover with following sauce.

½ pt double cream
¼ pt (or more) vodka
1 tablespoon of green peppercorns (not dried ones, but those in brine in a jar)

Add peppercorns to vodka and reduce. Add cream, reduce again - pour over meat (can be done in advance and reheated gently).

Mrs Ian Johnston
Kent

Butterflied Leg of Lamb

1 leg of lamb boned and split into a "butterfly"

Marinade:

¾ cup oil
½ cup chopped onion
2 tsp Dijon mustard
½ tsp oregano
½ tsp basil
¼ cup red wine vinegar (or red wine)
2 cloves garlic
2 tsp salt
Rosemary
1 bay leaf, ground pepper

Put marinade ingredients into plastic bag with butterflied leg of lamb and then into a bowl. Refrigerate for 24 - 48 hours, the longer the better. Barbecue flat side up for ten minutes, turn and baste and cook to taste (another 20 - 30 minutes probably). Lamb should be crusty on outside and pink inside. Slice and eat.

Annie Green
Kent

Out Hunting in the Bush

Before cooking, you will need to make your "stove" and "oven". Firstly, make a fire and place a flat iron stand over the fire. Dig a hole in the ground which must be deep enough to fit a large cast iron pot.

Hunting menu is as follows:

Chunky Tomato and Bacon Soup
Served with fresh bread

Roast Leg of Lamb
Served with roast potatoes, baked pumpkin and courgettes

Apple Pie
Make the bread first as this will take the longest:

1½ lb white flour
1 oz dried yeast
1 level tsp sugar
1½ lb wholemeal flour
3 tsp salt

Sieve the flour and salt into a warm basin - set aside in a warm place. Cream yeast and sugar in a jug and add part of the liquid (allow to stand for twenty minutes until soft). Make a well in the flour and add yeast mixture. Cover with a clean cloth and leave in the sun for fifteen minutes. Add the rest of the water to the flour. You may need more water to make a soft dough. Knead well until dough is smooth and leaves basin clean. Leave to rise, under a cloth, in the sun, then knead again. Repeat this process again. Form into loaves and put into warm greased loaf tins that have been lightly sprinkled with flour, leave for a little longer to rise.

Meanwhile collect hot coals from the fire and put them in the hole that you have dug. Place the cast iron pot with a lid in the hole and place coals on top. This is called the pre-heating oven! Finally put the loaves in the pot, making sure you don't get any ash on them. They will probably take thirty to fourty minutes. To check if they are ready, tip them upside down and bread should come out easily. Tap the bottom and it should sound hollow. Now wrap loaves in cloth until ready to use.

Before cooking the lamb, check the coals are still hot. Simply place the leg of lamb in the pot. Sprinkle with seasoning and fresh rosemary if you have any. Cover with lid and put more coals on top. Depending on the size, the lamb should take no longer than if you were using an electric oven.

The apple pie is prepared next. For this you will need ready made puff pastry and two tins apples. Grease a rectangular pastry tin, carefully put in your pastry, then fill with apples. Sprinkle the top with cinnamon. Beat an egg and brush edge of pastry before putting on the top layer. Trim edges and press down with a fork. Brush top of pastry with egg and prick with a fork. Make leaf shapes with any spare pastry and place artfully on top. This can go into the oven when lamb is cooked.

Soup

2 tbsp butter
2 onions
2 chicken stock cubes
15 tomatoes
6 bacon rashers, chopped
6 cups water
Salt and pepper

Over the fire, melt butter in a pan and add onions and bacon. Stir in peeled, seeded and chopped tomatoes, water and stock cubes. Season. Bring to the boil and simmer for twenty minutes.

Finally - The potatoes and vegetables:

Peel the potatoes and add to lamb, baste with juices from the lamb. Cut the pumpkin and wrap in tin foil and place around the fire. Cut the courgettes, place in water and bring to boil on the "stove". To check whether the lamb is cooked - pierce with a knife and the juices should run out a clear colour. If it is ready, wrap in foil and keep warm by the fire. Gravy can be made with the left over juices - add some flour and heat, making sure the mixture is smooth and lump free - add more water to get the consistency you require.

Now you can relax, have a cold beer and await the hunters' return.

Anne Freshman
Zimbabwe

Gigot à la Provençale

A leg or shoulder of lamb
2 onions
4 tomatoes
6 black olives
3 cloves garlic
2 aubergines
1 green pepper
Olive oil, salt, pepper and herbs

Cut cloves of garlic into slivers and push into small incisions made in the surface of the meat. Paint the joint with olive oil and put into a pre-heated oven gas 7 / 425°F. After 10 minutes, reduce the heat to gas 5 / 380°F. Baste. Chop the onions, slice the aubergines (previously cut into slices, sprinkled with salt and left to drain). Slice the green peppers and season with salt and pepper. Skin and chop the tomatoes and 45 minutes after putting the meat into the oven, add the chopped tomatoes, sliced aubergines and two cloves of garlic crushed. A few minutes before serving, stir in the stoned olives, cut into pieces and chopped herbs. Total cooking time for meat is 2 hours. Serve the joint on a large platter surrounded by it's rich wine-coloured sauce. It will need no gravy or green vegetable, just a purée of potatoes to accompany it and a green salad to follow.

Susan Mowll
Kent

Willingdon Steak

750 g / 1½ lb braising steak (cut into 4)
2 cloves garlic
100 g / 4 oz mushrooms
1 tbsp lemon juice
1 - 2 tbsp brandy
150 ml / ¼ pt single cream
1 onion
50 g / 2 oz butter
Salt and pepper
1 tbsp Worcester Sauce
150 ml / ¼ pt beef stock
1 tbsp parsley

1. Fry chopped onion and garlic in butter until soft.
2. Brown the steak on both sides.
3. Add brandy and flambé.
4. Add lemon juice, Worcester sauce, beef stock, seasoning; bring to the boil.
5. Place in ovenproof dish and cook 180°C / gas 4 for 1½ hours until tender.
6. Stir in cream and garnish with chopped parsley.

Jane Alvey
Sussex

Beef (or Venison) with Port and Guinness

6 lb venison shoulder or brisket of beef, cut into 1" squares
10 fl oz port
4 sprigs thyme
2 cloves crushed garlic
3 tbsp butter
3 level tbsp flour
2 pints Guinness
2 bay leaves
8 oz chopped onions
2 x 14 oz jars pickled walnuts
3 tbsp olive oil
Salt and black pepper

Night before, put meat in large bowl with bay leaves, thyme, Guinness and port with a plate on top. In a casserole, heat half the butter and oil. Drain meat and dry with kitchen paper and reserve juices etc. Brown a little at a time. Heat rest of butter and oil, add onions and garlic and cook for 10 minutes. Drain walnuts and cut into quarters. Return meat to casserole and stir in flour, pour in marinade mix, add walnuts and seasoning and bring to simmer. Put lid on and place into oven for three hours, at gas 1 - 2.

Mrs Victor Pope
Kent

Boeuf à la Bourguignonne

Serves 8

3 lb good stewing beef
12 - 16 baby onions, quartered
2 glasses red wine
Salt and pepper
Flour and oil or dripping
6 rashers bacon, best unsmoked
2 cloves garlic
½ lb button mushrooms
¾ pint beef stock
2 bay leaves

Cut beef in cubes. Chop bacon and sauté it in oil or dripping, then brown the onions and remove both. Brown the meat, sprinkling with a little flour and turning well. Transfer to casserole dish and add stock, wine, crushed garlic, bay leaves and seasoning. Simmer covered for at least 2 hours at 150°C / gas 2, adding a little more stock if necessary. About half an hour before serving, sauté the mushrooms in a little butter and add to casserole. Cook for another 15 minutes.

Anne Findlay
Kent

Beef Provençale

Serves 4

2 lb braising steak
2 leeks, sliced
14 oz can tomatoes
1 teaspoon dried thyme
1 beef stock cube
1 lb baby potatoes
1 tablespoon plain flour
2 oz butter
2 cloves garlic, crushed
2 bay leaves
1 cup water
1½ cups dry red wine
4 small courgettes
2 tablespoons water, extra

Cut fat and sinew from steak. Cut steak in bite-sized pieces. Melt butter in large saucepan, add steak and fry until well browned all over; remove from pan. Add leeks and garlic to pan, fry until leeks are lightly browned. Stir in undrained crushed tomatoes, bay leaves, thyme, water and crumbled stock cube, wine, potatoes and steak. Bring to the boil, reduce heat, cover and simmer for 40 minutes or until steak is tender. Add courgettes and cook for a further 10 minutes. Blend flour with extra water, stir over heat until mixture boils and thickens.

Alison Cahill
Essex

Beef Stroganoff

25 g butter
1 clove garlic - crushed
1 tbsp red wine
1 level tsp french mustard
Salt and pepper
1 dstsp finely chopped thyme
100 g tagliatelle
1 onion - sliced
250 g rump steak - cut into thin strips
50 g mushrooms - thinly sliced
75 g natural yoghurt
1 dstsp finely chopped parsley
Croutons of fried bread

1. Melt butter in a frying pan, add onions and garlic and fry until lightly browned.
2. Add steak to the pan and brown on all sides.
3. Add wine and simmer gently for 5 minutes to reduce the wine.

4. Add mushrooms, mustard, yoghurt and salt and pepper to taste. Simmer for 5 minutes.
5. Just before serving, stir in the herbs.
6. Garnish with croutons and serve with tagliatelle.

NB For a richer (and less healthy) sauce, substitute soured cream or crème fraîche for the yoghurt.

Cook tagliatelle in plenty of boiling water for approximately 5 minutes. Drain and serve immediately.

Lesley Pargeter
Ashford School

Tranche de Jambon Rose - Marie or Ham Slices in Cream Sauce

Serves 4 - 5

4 - 5 slices cooked ham, ¼ inch thick
1 dstsp oil
1 level tbsp flour
4 tbsp Madeira or sweet white wine
Ground black pepper
1 tbsp shallots or spring onions, finely chopped
1 oz butter
¼ pint double cream
¼ pint ham or chicken stock
1 tsp tomato purée

Trim excess fat from ham, pat dry. Heat butter and oil in large frying pan and fry ham slices a few at a time until lightly browned and set aside. Leave one tablespoon fat in pan and fry shallots or spring onions until soft then stir in the flour and cook, stirring for two minutes. Bring stock and Madeira or white wine to boil and blend into the shallots and flour. Add tomato purée and pepper. When simmering, stir in the cream and continue stirring for several minutes until sauce is a light coating consistency. Check seasoning, add ham slices and reheat gently. Especially good served on a bed of cooked chopped spinach. (I sometimes double up on the amount of sauce.)

Mrs James Woodhouse
Kent

Ham Baked with Coffee

1 ham
Herbs (bay leaf, parsley stalks, thyme)
4 heaped tbsp brown sugar
1 onion
2 flat tbsp ground neat coffee
1 heaped tsp made mustard

Soak ham overnight. Boil for 25 minutes per lb with herbs and onion. Leave to cool and then remove skin. Mix together into paste - coffee, sugar and mustard and plaster over ham. Bake in hot oven for 40 minutes.

(This is an old Irish country house recipe and delicious.)

Jennifer Dean
Kent

Jambon à la Bourgogne

Serves 4

12 thin slices cooked ham
7 oz tin chopped tomatoes
8 oz mushrooms
1 glassful port
8 oz Cheddar cheese
5 oz double cream or crème fraîche
1 oz butter

Slice and lightly fry mushrooms in butter. Grate cheese, place a sprinkling of grated cheese on each slice of ham and roll. Place rolled ham in an ovenproof dish, spread mushrooms over the ham - mix together tomatoes, cream and port, pour over and sprinkle remaining cheese on top. Place in a pre-heated oven 180°C / 350°F / gas 4 for approximately 40 - 45 minutes.

Penny Donaldson
Devon

Sausage Pie

Serves 4 - 6

Shortcrust pastry
4 tomatoes (skinned)
1 tablespoon brown sugar
1 lb thick sausages
Hard boiled eggs

Boil the sausages for 5 minutes. Then skin them and mash with the sugar. Line a pie dish with the pastry. Then place the sausage into the dish, cover this with the sliced tomatoes. Top with the sliced hard boiled eggs, then cover with the pastry. Decorate the top with leaves, cut from the left over pastry, then brush with milk. Cook in the oven for 20 - 25 minutes at 220°C. This dish can be served hot or cold.

James Lewis
London

Liver And Apple Potjie

In Southern Africa we cook on open fires and a 'Potjie' (pronounced 'poiqi') is a small cast iron pot, usually with three legs, that can be placed on the fire - or as in fact happens, the fires can be placed under the pot! A kind of stew is often made in potjies, with mutton, beef stewing meat, game stewing meat and also oxtail. A traditional potjie is not supposed to be stirred at all. First you put in your meat and when that starts tenderising a bit the rest of the ingredients (the veg) follow in layers. First the potatoes, because they take the longest time to cook and then the carrots, tomatoes, green beans etc. Remember to listen to the potjie. As soon as you cannot hear it you need to add more juice (wine makes excellent juice!) The following is cooked in a potjie but unlike the traditional dishes, this one can be stirred:

½ kg liver (chopped into slithers)
4 onions (chopped)
1 tbsp salt
3 cloves
500 ml sherry
250 ml double cream
250 g bacon strips
3 garlic cloves (chopped)
Black pepper to taste
6 cooking apples (cut in cm squares)
500 g fresh mushrooms (chopped)

1. First fry the onions in a bit of cooking oil until they just start browning - take out of oil and keep separate.
2. Fry liver, garlic, cloves and bacon until brown.
3. Add fried onions, apples, cream and sherry.
4. Cook over low heat for about an hour or until the apples are soft.
5. Taste throughout the process and add salt, pepper etc.
6. Serve with cooked, crushed corn.

Sanet Van Wyk
Namibia

Liver Stroganoff

Serves 4

1 lb (450 g) lambs' liver
Oil for frying
3 rashers chopped, streaky bacon
¼ pint stock
5 oz (142 g) yoghurt or soured cream
1 oz (20 g) seasoned flour
1 chopped onion
¼ lb (100 g) sliced mushrooms
Salt and pepper

Cut liver into half inch, 5 cm strips. Toss in seasoned flour. Heat oil in pan and fry liver till lightly browned. Remove from pan with slotted spoon and keep it warm. Fry onion, bacon and mushrooms. Add any remaining flour. Add stock. Bring it to the boil. Add the liver and season. Simmer for 5 minutes. Before serving, add yoghurt or cream and serve with pasta or rice.

Fiona Macey
Kent

Liver With Macaroni

¼ lb macaroni, boiled
4 rashers bacon
Tin Campbells mushroom soup
¾ lb liver (lamb or calves)
Onion

Fry the onion, bacon and liver. Chop into small pieces and add to macaroni. Pour over the tin of soup and a quarter of a pint of water. Put in oven to cook through. A very easy and a good supper dish.

Sue Webster
London

Chapter 5

Main Courses Poultry

Chicken Parmesan with Basil

Serves 4

4 large chicken fillets
1/3 cup grated Parmesan cheese
3 rashers bacon
2 cloves garlic
½ tsp dry mustard
1 cup fresh breadcrumbs
1 tbsp chopped parsley
90 g butter
1 tsp Worcestershire sauce

Basil Sauce:

1/3 cup oil
1 clove garlic
1/3 cup cream
Salt and pepper
¼ cup white vinegar
1 cup fresh basil leaves
1 egg yolk

Combine in bowl breadcrumbs cheese and parsley. Chop bacon finely and fry in pan until crisp. Drain. Add bacon to breadcrumb mixture. Melt butter in saucepan, add crushed garlic, Worcestershire sauce and dry mustard. Mix well. Dip chicken fillets in butter mixture and place in shallow ovenproof dish. Press crumb mixture on top of each fillet. Bake, uncovered, in moderate oven 20 to 25 minutes. Serve with basil sauce.

Basil sauce:

Combine in saucepan oil, vinegar, crushed garlic, finely chopped fresh basil leaves and cream, stir until heated through. Add egg yolk and stir until sauce thickens. Do not boil. Season with salt and pepper.

Caroline Armstrong-Jones
London

Chicken Liver Risotto

1 large onion
2 cups rice (Uncle Ben's will do)
1 cup chicken livers
5 cups chicken stock
Olive or other oil (about a large tablespoon but big pans use more)

Chop the onion and fry in the oil until soft but not brown. Chop the chicken livers roughly and fry them too until no longer red. Add the rice and fry that as well mixing up the whole lot and after about two minutes add the stock. Close the pan and cook on medium heat until all the stock has been absorbed. Add the salt and pepper to taste (it depends on what the stock tastes like!) and serve with a green salad. This will feed about 5 people and is an economical dish and quick to make.

Judy Tren
South Africa

Chicken and Avocado Casserole

Serves 6

2 avocado pears peeled, stoned and sliced

6 chicken joints / pieces	40 g / 1½ oz flour
Salt and pepper	1 tbsp chopped fresh thyme
Grated rind and juice of 1 lemon	125 ml / ¼ pt soured cream
50 g / 2 oz butter	2 onions, chopped
250 ml / ½ pt white wine	125 ml / ¼ pt chicken stock

Coat the chicken joints / pieces with the flour, seasoned with salt and pepper, chopped thyme and lemon rind. Melt the butter in a large frying pan and fry chicken pieces on all sides until golden brown. Remove from the pan and place in a casserole. Fry onions in the fat remaining in pan for 5 minutes. Sprinkle over remaining flour. Cook for 1 minute and then gradually stir in the wine and stock. Bring to the boil stirring all the time. Pour over the chicken. Cover, cook at 180°C / 350°F / gas 4 for 1 hour. Allow to cool for a minute then stir in the soured cream. Toss the avocado slices in lemon juice. Add to the chicken.

Note: If wishing to freeze this dish, do so before cream and pears are added. Reheat and then add soured cream and pears as above.

Marilla Blenkin
Kent

Breasts of Chicken Stuffed with Ginger, Lime and Almonds

Serves 4

4 chicken breasts skinned and boned
2 oz ground almonds
4 tbsp jellied chicken stock
3 oz butter
8 almonds blanched and slivered
2 tbsp double cream
1 square inch piece of fresh ginger peeled and grated
1 lime - zest grated finely and juice squeezed

Cut a pocket in the side of each breast with a very sharp knife big enough to take one and a half heaped tablespoons butter stuffing. Soften 2 oz of butter and blend in the grated ginger, half of the grated lime zest, the juice of the lime and the ground almonds. Divide this savoury butter evenly between the chicken pockets. Close the pockets with a toothpick and season all over with salt and freshly ground pepper. Chill until the butter is quite firm. Melt the remaining 1 oz butter in a shallow pan and cook breasts on both sides until golden. Cover with greaseproof paper and cook at gas 4 / 350°F for 15 minutes. Transfer to hot dish. Add almonds to pan and cook in remaining butter until golden. Stir in remaining zest, lime juice and chicken stock mixing well together. Remove from heat and stir in cream. Season well with salt and pepper and pour sauce over chicken.

Priscilla Eagles
Kent

Chicken Breasts in Garlic Crisps

Serves 6

Very easy and delicious:

6 skinless chicken breasts
3 cloves garlic
Handful chopped parsley
2 large packets salted crisps
3 - 4 oz butter
Black pepper

Place chicken breasts in an ovenproof dish. Melt the butter in a pan and add the crushed garlic, crushed crisps and parsley. Mix thoroughly and season with pepper. Spread the mixture over the chicken breasts and bake in the oven at 375°F / 190°C / gas 4. Place it in the bottom right of the Aga for 40 minutes. Serve with green salad.

Carolyn Hill
Wiltshire

Indian Chicken

1 chicken, jointed
2 tsp finely grated ginger
1 tsp paprika
2 tbsp lemon juice
2 tbsp oil (sesame if possible)
Chilli powder
Stock made from giblets
2 cloves garlic, crushed
1½ tbsp curry powder
1 tsp garam masala
2 tsp soy sauce
2 tbsp flour
Hot chilli sauce to taste
Salt & pepper

1. Combine all ingredients (except chicken) to make a paste.
2. Rub paste over chicken joints.
3. Leave for at least an hour, or overnight.
4. Pour over sufficient stock for gravy.
5. Bake at 180°C for about 1 hour, covered.

Penny Hodson
Nottinghamshire

Hot Chicken Salad

4 cups cooked chicken
4 tbsp lemon juice
1 green pepper
1 cup grated cheese
1 cup / 8 oz salad cream
4 cups celery
Large onion
1 can condensed chicken soup
2 cups crisps
1 tsp salt

Fry onion and pepper. Mix the chicken, celery, soup, salad cream, lemon juice and salt. Butter a dish. Crush crisps with cheese. Sprinkle on top. Bake 350°F for 25 minutes.

Hillery De Pover
Kent

Chicken with Mustard and Honey

10 chicken pieces (preferably thighs with no skin)
1 tsp curry powder
1 tbsp coarse grain mustard
80 g butter
½ cup cream
1 tsp stock powder
2 tbsp honey
2 tsp lemon juice
1 tsp seasoned salt

Melt butter and add salt, curry powder, stock powder, mustard and honey. Place chicken in a single layer and pour this over and leave for 2 - 3 hours. Then bake in a moderate oven for 1½ hours covered. When done remove the chicken pieces and soak up the excess fat off the sauce with paper towels. Then boil it to reduce and thicken a bit, add the lemon juice and cream - don't boil again and pour over the chicken and serve.

Judy Tren
South Africa

Chicken Lima

Serves 6

2 x 2½ lb chickens
Pieces of vegetable and herbs

Sauce:

1 small onion, chopped
1 tsp paprika
1 heaped tsp tomato purée
1 small glass port
¼ pt lightly whipped cream
1 dstsp curry powder
½ pt of stock - perhaps a little less
1 slice lemon
¼ pt mayonnaise

Salad:

½ lb rice
1 green pepper
4 oz french beans

Poach chickens with water and add vegetables and herbs to flavour until tender. Cool in liquid. Prepare sauce. Soften onion in oil. Add curry powder and after 2 minutes the paprika. Cook for a few seconds then add stock, purée and lemon. Simmer for 5 - 7 minutes, then strain. Add port and when cool beat into the mayonnaise with the cream and a pinch of sugar (the mayonnaise must be thick). Boil the rice, drain. Dice the cucumber and blanch the peppers, (the cucumber salted after chopping and the liquid poured off before using). Add the cooked beans and moisten with a french dressing. Carve chicken and arrange at one end of the plate, coat with sauce. Pile the rice mixture at the other end. Garnish with watercress or parsley or red peppers or chives.

Marilla Blenkin
Kent

Chicken Salad in a Curried Ring

Curried Ring:

1 tin condensed chicken soup (make up with 1 pint of water)
1 tin pimentos diced, (or tomatoes with insides removed)
½ oz gelatine
1 teacup mayonnaise
2 celery sticks diced
Salt and pepper
1 dstsp curry powder
1 small onion finely grated
4 hard boiled eggs chopped

Measure a quarter of a pint of soup into the saucepan and sprinkle on gelatine and soak for a few minutes. Slowly heat and dissolve, then stir in the remaining soup, mayonnaise, onion and salt and pepper. Cool and stir when it starts to thicken then fold in pimento, eggs and celery. Pour into ring mould and set in fridge.

Chicken Salad:

Mix together about 3 - 4 cooked chicken joints cut into small pieces, about 4 tablespoons mayonnaise, 2 celery sticks diced, chopped spring onions (optional), lemon juice, salt and pepper. Add about ¼ lb white grapes and ½ oz of toasted flaked almonds. Pour mixture into centre of mould. When turned out, decorate with lettuce leaves.

Caroline Loder-Symonds
Kent

Lemon Chicken

6 chicken pieces
2 tbsp butter
½ tsp salt
1 tsp grated lemon rind
½ tsp sugar
Large pinch garlic powder
Small pinch cayenne pepper
2 tbsp cooking oil
½ cup lemon juice
½ tsp pepper
¼ cup salad oil
½ tsp paprika
Large pinch dry mustard

Season chicken pieces with a little salt and pepper. Heat butter and cooking oil together and fry the chicken until evenly browned. Pour any remaining fat out of the pan. Put all remaining ingredients into a screwtop jar and shake until blended well. Pour this mixture over chicken pieces, cover pan and simmer gently for about 30 - 40 minutes.

Norma Rattray
Natal

Chicken in Barbecue Sauce

Serves 6

6 chicken joints

Sauce:

1 onion
1 level tsp salt
4 level tbsp soft brown sugar
2 tsp made mustard
Juice of ½ lemon
½ pt water
1 tbsp oil
Freshly milled pepper
1 level tbsp cornflour
1 tsp Worcester sauce
2½ oz can tomato purée

Brown chicken by wrapping in foil and putting into oven, or heat some butter in a frying pan and fry gently to brown. Place in a casserole. Peel and finely chop the onion. Heat oil in a saucepan and cook gently until the onion is tender. Measure remaining ingredients for sauce into a basin. Blend well and add to the onion in the pan. Stir to mix and bring up to the boil and simmer for 5 minutes. Draw pan off the heat and pour sauce over the chicken joints.

Cover the casserole and cook in the centre of a moderate oven 180°C / 350°F / gas 4 and cook for 1 hour. Serve with plain boiled rice.

Mrs Charlie Simkins
Kent

Pot Roast Chicken with Tomatoes and Garlic

A big pot with lid
A handful of fresh herbs
1 lb ripe tomatoes
2 cloves garlic
1 large chicken
Olive oil
1 large onion
¼ pt dry white wine

Preheat oven to 350°F / gas 4. Put chicken in a large pot or pan. Add some olive oil depending on your taste. You can leave this out. Tuck herbs around chicken. Core tomatoes and cut in half. Chop and slice onion and garlic. Put everything in the pot. Season with salt and pepper. Cook for 1¼ - 1½ hours. Serve with french bread and a huge salad.

Mrs Pennright

Left Over Chicken with Sherry

2 egg yolks, beaten
2 fl oz sherry
1½ lb cooked chicken
8 fl oz single cream
2 tsp finely grated lemon rind

Put the egg yolks in the heatproof bowl. Beat in the cream, lemon rind and sherry. Put the bowl over a pan of water and cook, stirring constantly, for three minutes or until the sauce thickens slightly.

Arrange chicken pieces in a serving dish and pour the sauce over them. Chill in the fridge for 30 minutes before serving.

Anne Crossley
Norfolk

Chicken Satay

Serves 4 as main course or 20 as cocktails

4 chicken breasts - skinned
1 small jar runny honey
Coriander - to taste, fresh or ground
1 jar smooth peanut butter
1 small carton soured cream / yoghurt
Ginger - to taste, fresh or ground

Chop chicken breasts into cubes, each about half an inch square. Put into a bowl. Mix all other ingredients together (using initially half a jar of peanut butter and adding more to your own taste. It should be of coating consistency). Cover chicken. Leave to marinade for as long as possible. Skewer chicken. For cocktail bits - half pieces per stick, if main course - more. Place in hot oven for 20 - 30 minutes. Grill, possibly, to give colour before serving. If there is any marinade left over, pour over before grilling. Serve. If you soak skewers overnight in a bowl of water they are less likely to burn and snap.

Sally Everist
London

Hot Chicken Salad

4 chicken breasts
4 spring onions
Salt and pepper
4 oz grated cheese
1 jar mayonnaise (preferably Hellmans)
4 sticks celery
2 courgettes
½ tsp paprika
1 large pack plain crisps

Loosely cover chicken breasts with foil and bake in oven. Meanwhile, chop celery, spring onions and courgettes into bite sized pieces. Grate the cheese and crush the crisps, mix these two together for the topping. When the chicken is cooked, chop into bite sized pieces, add to spring onions etc, then stir in the jar of mayonnaise, season to taste. Place in ovenproof dish, cover with the crisps and cheese and warm through in oven for 10 minutes. Delicious served with hot new potatoes and green salad.

Fiona Hughes D'Aeth
Dorset

Chicken à l'Eden

Serves 4

4 chicken breasts - sliced
4 cloves garlic - crushed
1 tin flagelot beans - rinsed
½ pt cream
2 onions - sliced
¼ lb mushrooms - sliced
½ pt white wine

Sweat the onions and garlic in a little oil, add mushrooms then chicken, stir well and add the wine. Reduce and add the cream and flagelot beans, bring to the boil making sure the chicken is thoroughly cooked, then season.

Amanda Gow
Kent

Chicken Jade

Serves 4 - 6

A 3½ lb chicken or approximately 2 lb cooked chicken or turkey meat
½ lb chopped mushrooms
2 cloves garlic
2 jars Baxters Stroganoff Sauce
2 oz butter
1 large chopped onion
½ pt double cream
2 tsp mace
Good measure brandy

Cook the chicken in a microwave and take meat off the bone, or chop up cooked meat. Soften the chopped onion and garlic in butter. Add mushrooms. Add sauce, mace, cream and brandy and heat gently - do not boil. Add the chicken to this mixture.

Can be served immediately or kept in the fridge to be reheated in the oven or microwave.

This dish is named for my granddaughter. If she is staying with me I don't have much time for cooking!

Chris Bainbridge
Kent

Tandoori Chicken

Serves 4

2½ - 3½ lb chicken cut into pieces
1 piece fresh ginger (walnut size)
3 cloves garlic
½ heaped tsp chilli powder
½ tsp salt
Drop of red colouring
5 oz carton plain yoghurt
½ good size onion, finely chopped
1 heaped tsp cumin powder
1 heaped tsp Tandoori mix powder
½ tsp black pepper

Put all of the above ingredients in a liquidiser or Magimix - (but not the chicken pieces). Put the chicken pieces (well slashed) into a bowl and cover with the yoghurt mix. Leave it for anything up to 24 hours. Pre-heat grill and grill the chicken pieces well at first then more gently until they are cooked on both sides. They will blacken a little as cooked.

Serve with raw onion and tomato salad (tomatoes cut into chunks with some oil and vinegar dressing). Also perhaps plain yoghurt with thinly sliced cucumber and mint.

Anne Neame
Kent

Sweet Gingered Chicken

8 level tbsp apricot jam
8 level tbsp dry sherry
2 cloves garlic crushed
12 oz aubergine
5 level tbsp soy sauce
2 level tbsp lemon juice
1 inch root ginger finely chopped
6 chicken breasts with skin

Mix first four ingredients together. Add garlic and ginger. Thinly slice aubergine and line a roasting tin (largish) with foil. Spread out aubergine and chicken pieces on foil in tin. Spoon ginger mixture over the contents. Cook at 220°C for about 30 minutes, basting occasionally until chicken pieces are well glazed and brown. Add a little water if necessary towards the end of the cooking.

Anne Neame
Kent

Chicken in Gruyère, Tarragon Sauce

1 chicken
Chopped tarragon
Butter
Salt and pepper

Sauce:

2 oz butter
¼ pt stock from giblets
½ pt double cream
2 - 3 tsp chopped tarragon
Salt and freshly ground black pepper
2½ oz flour
Wine glass white wine
2 - 3 tsp Dijon mustard
2 tbsp (at least) grated Gruyère
Breadcrumbs for topping

1. Roast a nice plump chicken in butter with tarragon and butter stuffing. When cool carve into several good sized pieces.
2. Make a stock from the giblets cooked in white wine, onions, leeks and carrots.
3. Make a thickish white sauce using stock, double cream and white wine and add fresh chopped tarragon, grated Gruyère, grey Poupon Dijon mustard, salt and black pepper. Make the sauce slowly and allow to mature. When ready pour over chicken pieces, top with more grated Gruyère and breadcrumbs and a little of the chicken juices. Put in a very hot oven for 5 - 10 minutes and finish under grill so it is golden brown. Serve with new potatoes and fresh green vegetables.

Katie Gunn
Kent

Chicken Charter Pie

Dice chicken and fry slowly until cooked through. Place in dish. Add fried, chopped onions, sweetcorn, sliced mushrooms and quartered hard boiled eggs. Season. Pour in double cream to cover about half way up the dish. Cover with puff pastry and cook in the oven for 40 minutes.

Sue Webster
London

Chicken Breast with Garlic and Ginger

Serves 4

Preparation and cooking time: 15 mins

500 g (1 lb) boneless chicken breasts, skinned
5 cm (2 inch) piece of fresh ginger, peeled and grated
4 tbsp olive oil
2 garlic cloves, crushed
2 tbsp soy sauce
¼ tsp chilli powder
Mange tout, topped and tailed
6 spring onions, chopped finely
2 tbsp white wine

Cut the chicken into thin strips and stir fry for a minute or so in the hot oil, tossing all the time so that they become well coated. Add the rest of the ingredients and continue stir frying for a further 3 - 4 minutes, being careful not to let the chicken become dry. Serve immediately with boiled rice or egg noodles.

Jan Francis

Spinach Stuffed Chicken with a Tomato Puddle

1 lb cooked fresh or frozen chopped leaf spinach
6 boneless chicken breasts
2 onions
3 cloves garlic, crushed
Salt and black pepper
1 lb de-rinded smoked streaky bacon
1 tbsp tomato purée
Butter
Tin plum tomatoes

Beat out the chicken breasts between two pieces of greaseproof paper with a rolling pin, until double the size. Fry one onion and two cloves of garlic in some butter until soft. Add the spinach and mix together, season well. Divide the mixture between the chicken breasts, but don't overfill. Roll up the chicken breasts. Stretch out the de-rinded bacon with the back of a knife and wrap around the chicken. Place in an ovenproof dish with the join on the bottom. Bake at 400°F / 170°C for 45 minutes or until crispy. Take out, slice thinly and place 4 - 5 slices on each plate. Also delicious cold.

For The Tomato Puddle:

Fry remaining onion in garlic until soft and add the tomatoes and tomato purée and season. Simmer for half an hour and purée in a blender.

Sara Hurst
London

Chicken in Cider Sauce with Mushrooms

3¼ lb chicken
2 onions, peeled and chopped
Milk
2 oz flour
½ pt dry cider
Salt and freshly ground black pepper
2 oz butter
6 oz mushrooms, cleaned and quartered

Put chicken and giblets in small roasting tin or casserole. Add cider, onion and seasoning. Cover and cook in moderate oven for 1½ hours. Lift chicken out to cool and strain remaining stock. Skim off fat and make up to 1¼ pints with milk. Remove chicken meat from carcase and cut into bite sized pieces. Melt butter in pan, add flour, cook and stir in stock and milk. Bring to the boil, stirring, and allow to thicken. Add mushrooms and cook for 5 minutes. Taste and adjust seasoning. Stir in chicken, cook for 45 minutes, gas 4.

Di McKenzie
Kent

Quick Chicken

8 portions chicken
2 cloves garlic
Salt and pepper
Tomatoes, aubergines, mushrooms (optional)
2 onions
Butter

Place chicken, onion, garlic, salt and pepper in layers in ovenproof dish together with the optional vegetables. Dot with butter and cook in hot oven for ¾ hour. Serve with bacon rolls for extra oomph. Perfect for those occasions when preparation time is limited.

Catherine McCully
Kent

Eastern Chicken

1 pkt chicken thighs
1 cup chicken stock
Half cup blackcurrants (optional)
1 cup chopped green pepper
Pepper
1/3 cup flour
410 g tomato purée
2.5 - 3 tsp curry powder
1 cup chopped onions
2 tsp salt
Half teaspoon thyme

Blend herbs, salt and pepper, curry powder and flour in bowl with lid. Add chicken to mixture and shake well. Place in casserole. Add onions and green pepper, mix around chicken pieces. Add stock then tomato purée. Mix altogether. Sprinkle currants on top. Cook for two hours at 330°F / 150°C.

Wendy Hartley
Natal

Chicken and Mushroom Filo Parcel

Serves 8

8 small skinless and boneless chicken breasts
3 oz (75 g) butter plus 1½ oz melted butter
2 medium onions chopped
½ pt (275 ml) dry white wine
1 tsp pesto (optional)
Salt and pepper
8 oz (225 g) mushrooms sliced thinly
8 oz (225 g) cream cheese
2 tbsp chopped parsley
6 sheets filo pastry, defrosted

Cut the chicken breasts into half inch slices. Sauté the chicken in 2 oz of butter until golden, remove from pan. Add extra 1 oz of butter and fry onions gently until soft. Turn up heat slightly, add mushrooms and cook for a further 5 - 6 minutes. Add wine and simmer until wine is reduced by half. Add cream cheese and stir until it is smooth and blended in. Return chicken to pan and add pesto and parsley, mix well and season to taste. Butter a 9 inch loose-bottomed cake tin. Take sheets of filo pastry singly and line tin overlapping slightly each time, leaving the ends of sheets hanging down outside the tin. Gently spoon the chicken mixture into the tin and fold ends of pastry over the top to enclose chicken. Brush the top with melted butter. Place in centre of preheated oven for 25 minutes 180°C / 350°F / gas 4. Then carefully remove sides of tin, brush sides of the pastry with remaining melted butter and return to oven for a further 20 minutes or until it is golden brown all over. Transfer to serving dish and serve hot.

Delicious with a green salad!

Diana Tosswill
London

Chicken with Leeks and Cream (a quick and easy supper dish)

Serves 4

4 - 5 chicken breasts
4 - 5 medium sized leeks
3 oz butter
Dry sherry
1 - 2 shallots, diced
¾ lb medium sized white mushrooms
6 oz approx single cream
Herbs
A heavy pan (eg; a Le Creuset casserole is ideal)

Cook the thinly sliced leeks in about half the butter, after about 5 minutes add the shallots and cook for another 5 - 10 minutes according to your taste. Add the sliced and halved mushrooms and cook until tender. Take off the heat. Fry the chicken breasts, cut into inch size cubes, very quickly in the rest of the butter with some herbs and when sealed add to the vegetables. Add the sherry, a small or large amount according to taste. This can now be left to cook on a low heat for half an hour or more as suits the chef. Add the cream a little while before serving and bring back to full heat. As its only single cream you can boil it a little without spoiling. If supper is delayed add more cream and sherry.

Please note all ingredients can be very approximate.

Nicola Armitage
Kent

Chicken in Peanut Sauce

4 chicken breasts
1 pint milk
Half jar peanut butter (smooth)
1 pint chicken stock

Lightly fry chicken on both sides and put in casserole. Make chicken stock. Put it in a saucepan with 1 pint of milk and the half jar of peanut butter. Heat until peanut butter has dissolved. Pour over chicken and cook in a medium oven for 30 minutes.

Annie Owen
Kent

Turkey with Mozzarella and Ham

1 turkey breast (approx 1¼ lb)
6 slices ham
4 shallots
¼ lb mushrooms
6 oz Mozzarella cheese
4 cloves garlic
2 tbsp olive oil
½ pt double cream

Make six cuts in turkey breast not quite the whole way through. Place a slice of ham and a slice of Mozzarella cheese in each slice. Place turkey in roasting tin with garlic and shallots and pour over olive oil. Roast for one hour in oven 180°C / 375°F basting several times. Remove meat and keep warm. Add mushrooms to pan and cook quickly on top of stove. Remove mushrooms, and place around turkey. With a wooden spoon, mush up shallots and garlic in pan. Add cream and bring to boil mixing all the time. Pour sauce over turkey and serve separately.

Mrs Jack Sherston
Kent

Chapter 6

Main Courses
Game

Pheasant Bentley

Serves 4

1 pheasant
2 large onions
3 tbsp cream
4 oz streaky bacon
1 beaten egg
2 oz butter
2 tbsp flour
2 cloves garlic
3 oz breadcrumbs
Half pint white wine

Put pheasant in pan with 1 oz butter, half the onions (chopped), garlic and wine. Cook 1¾ hours. Chop bacon, fry until crisp, add breadcrumbs and stir till brown. Put aside. Bone, skin and roughly shred pheasant meat and put in a shallow dish. Chop rest of onions and cook in remaining butter. Stir in the flour. Strain stock from pheasant and stir half a pint of liquid into onion mixture. Cook slowly for 10 minutes. Put in Magimix. Mix beaten egg with cream. Gradually add into sauce. Pour over pheasant. Sprinkle with breadcrumb mixture and put in oven to heat through and crisp on top.

Mrs Michael Gatenby
London

Pheasant Breasts with Mushroom and Bacon Sauce

Serves 6

6 pheasant breasts, boned
4 oz streaky bacon, chopped
4 oz onion, skinned and chopped
½ pint pheasant or chicken stock
1 bay leaf
6 thick round slices bread
4 tbsp flour
4 oz mushrooms, wiped and sliced
8 tbsp red wine (approx)
4 oz butter
5 fl oz fresh single cream
Fresh watercress as garnish

Dust the pheasant breasts with flour and melt 1½ oz butter in frying pan. Gently brown pheasant breasts on all sides and then remove to a large casserole. Add the wine to the pan and bring to the boil, then pour over the pheasant. Melt 1½ oz butter, fry the bacon, mushrooms and onion slowly until onion starts to brown. Blend in three level tablespoons flour and stir in the stock. Add the bay leaf and pour the sauce over the pheasant. Cook in oven at

160°C for about 1½ hours. When pheasant is cooked remove from casserole. Remove bay leaf from sauce and purée the sauce in a Magimix. At same time fry bread in remaining butter. Drain and keep hot. Add fresh cream to the sauce, season and gently reheat. On a large dish, arrange each pheasant breast on a piece of fried bread and pour over sauce. Garnish with watercress and serve the remaining sauce in a jug.

Camilla Pascal
Kent

Pheasant Macaroni

2 cooked pheasants
2 cloves garlic
A few mushrooms
9 - 10 oz macaroni
2 onions
6 - 8 oz streaky bacon
1 glass wine

Béchamel sauce, using:

1 pt milk
2 oz butter
¼ pt yoghurt
2 oz flour
2 oz grated cheese
A few breadcrumbs

Cut off the pheasants legs and use for another recipe. Strip remaining meat from the birds and make the stock with the bones. Sauté the chopped onions, chopped garlic cloves, bacon cut into matchsticks and chopped or sliced mushrooms. Pour the wine over and let it cook until most of the liquid has gone. Add a quarter of a pint of the pheasant stock and a few mixed herbs and stir in and cook for about 20 minutes. Add pheasant meat cut into chunks. Cook the macaroni and arrest cooking by plunging it into cold water. Make the sauce and stir in the cheese, followed by the yoghurt. Season with salt and pepper and nutmeg. Mix in the macaroni. Put half the macaroni into a flattish dish, cover with the pheasant mixture and finish with the remaining macaroni. To reheat for serving - scatter coarse, slightly stale breadcrumbs all over the surface and bake at 375°F / 190°C / gas 5, top oven of Aga and shelf for about 45 minutes.

Mrs Charles Dawes
Kent

Pheasant Alsacienne

Serves 4

Pheasant (or chicken) joints
¼ pt strong stock (cube will do)
1½ oz butter
3 tbsp thick cream
Arrowroot to thicken
8 oz button mushrooms
1½ glasses white wine
1 dstsp oil
Squeeze of lemon
Seasoning
2½ oz paté (I use M & S chicken liver in carton)
Parsley and fried bread triangles to garnish

Melt oil and butter in sauté pan and arrange joints skin down. Season, and cook gently for about 15 minutes, turning occasionally. Then add half the stock and wine with the washed mushrooms and cook till tender. Dish bird and keep warm. Then add remaining liquid to pan. Thicken with arrowroot then blend the paté with a little of the liquid, the cream and a good squeeze of lemon. Adjust seasoning and pour over the joints, garnish and serve.

The measurements may need adjusting here and there to taste! The sauce is rich so I serve it with creamed mashed potatoes and a plain green vegetable.

Libby Cox
Kent

Pheasant in Cream

1 or 2 pheasants
1 wineglass brandy
½ pt cream
3 - 4 oz butter
Rich stock
Seasoning

Brown pheasants in butter in a heavy pan and season. Finish cooking with lid on, in a medium oven, basting often, for about 40 minutes. Take pheasant out, carve into portions and keep warm whilst sauce is made. Add brandy, stock and cream to pan juices, reduce by simmering for 5 minutes, stirring all the time. Pour over pheasant. Serve with mashed potatoes or rice. Can be made in advance and reheated gently.

Mrs Ian Johnston
Kent

Pheasant Dish

Pheasant - roasted
Bacon
Chopped nuts
Cream
White sauce
Breadcrumbs
Sherry
Daddies OK sauce

Make the white sauce and add sherry, cream and Daddies OK sauce to taste. Mix pheasant and sauce. Top with bacon, breadcrumbs and nuts. Put in oven to heat up and grill the top.

Sue Webster
London

Pheasant Bonne Femme

2 pheasants
1 glass water
6 rashers back bacon
1 oz butter
1 glass white wine
4 tbsp butter
½ lb mushrooms
Juice of ½ lemon

White Sauce:

2 oz butter
5 tbsp double cream
2 oz flour

Hollandaise Sauce:

4 egg yolks
6 oz boiling water
1 tbsp lemon juice
1 tbsp hot water

Smear pheasants all over with butter and put three pieces of bacon on each bird. Place in roasting tin with wine and water and cook for 1 hour in oven 180°C / 375°F. Baste often. Meanwhile sauté mushrooms with butter and lemon juice. Cut and pull meat into pieces and put in gratin dish. Make white sauce with 2 oz butter, 2 oz flour, pheasant juices and 5 tablespoons cream and pour over pheasant. Cover with mushrooms and bacon cut into small pieces. Make Hollandaise sauce by placing egg yolks in Magimix with lemon juice. Turn on. Gradually add boiling water and at the end, hot water. Pour onto dish and cook 20 minutes until hot and bubbly, 190°C / 400°F.

Mrs Jack Sherston
Kent

Pheasant in Savoury Sauce

1 cooked pheasant (or left overs)
½ pt milk
¼ pt stock or pheasant gravy
1 oz raisins
1 tbsp red currant jelly
2 oz butter
¼ pt red wine
Salt and pepper
1 onion, peeled and chopped
3 - 4 rashers streaky bacon, chopped

Fry onions and bacon in butter till lightly browned. Add flour and cook 1 - 2 minutes, blend in milk, wine and stock. Bring back to boil. Season and add raisins and red current jelly. Remove meat from carcass, chop into bite sized pieces (use carcass for stock). Stir meat into sauce, and reheat thoroughly. Serve with rice.

Mrs John Martin
Kent

Pheasant Casserole

1 pheasant jointed
1 oz butter
2 oz flour
Thinly peeled rind of one orange
1 tbsp redcurrant jelly
Bay leaf
1 tbsp oil
2 sliced onions
¾ pint stock
Juice of one orange
¼ pint port
Salt and pepper

Heat oil and butter. Fry pheasant joints quickly and put to one side. Fry onions until soft. Stir in flour and brown. Add stock and simmer for 2 - 3 minutes. Add orange juice and rind, red currant jelly, port and bay leaf. Simmer till the jelly has dissolved. Add salt and pepper. Place pheasant and sauce in casserole and cook in moderate oven till pheasant is tender. Times vary depending on the age of the pheasant. This freezes beautifully.

Caroline Loder-Symonds
Kent

Pigeon with Prunes

4 plump woodpigeons
3 oz chopped onion
8 rashers streaky bacon
Medium sized tin prunes

5 oz double cream
2 oz butter
¾ pint red wine
1½ oz flour

Soften the onion for ten minutes in a little butter. Put into a casserole (which should be large enough to hold the pigeons). Brown the pigeons in the rest of the butter and put into the casserole. Sprinkle with salt and freshly ground black pepper and cover each bird with two rashers of bacon. Pour in the red wine, cover and place in a hot oven for ten minutes then lower the heat to about gas one. Cook for a further four hours by which time the flesh should be starting to part from the breast bone. Place the pigeons on a clean dish. Skim fat off the sauce and thicken with a roux made from one and a half ounces of flour and an ounce of butter. Add chopped bacon and the drained and stoned prunes. If the gravy seems too thick, add a quarter of a pint of chicken stock and finally the double cream. Add salt and pepper to taste and pour over the pigeons and serve with potatoes in their jackets and a green vegetable.

Lynette Pearson
W Sussex

Casserole of Guinea Fowl

Serves 4

1 Guinea fowl
1 cup cream
3 tbsp Worcestershire sauce
2 tbsp lemon juice
2 tbsp french mustard
250 g sliced mushrooms
1 cup milk
1½ cups diced apple
1 tbsp brown sugar
1 tsp celery salt

Cut the bird into serving portions. Place in a pressure cooker with all the ingredients and cook for at least one hour. For a really superb taste, cook for the first hour, place in the fridge overnight and then re-cook for another hour the following day.

As I am a throw-in cook, your recipe might not taste as mine does. I can only give approximate measures!

Diana Runge
Natal

Guinea Fowl avec Sauce Normande

1 Guinea fowl
2 onions
Glass of Calvados
2 apples
½ bottle dry cider
Crème cru - small pot

In a large saucepan melt butter and oil and when hot, brown Guinea fowl all over. Add sliced apples and onions and cider. Cover and cook slowly for approximately 40 minutes. Remove Guinea fowl, joint and set aside to keep warm. Liquidise apples and onions and cider and return to saucepan. Add calvados and crème cru and season to taste. Pour sauce over Guinea fowl.

Peeled, cooked chestnuts served with this are delicious.

Mrs Peter Alliott
France

Lapin aux Pruneaux (Rabbit with Prunes)

Serves 4

10 or 12 prunes
12 very small onions
1 large rabbit cut into 8 pieces
Salt and black pepper
2 tbsp flour
Bouquet garni (1 sprig parsley, thyme, bay leaf)
½ lb (227 g) slab bacon
227 g button mushrooms
4 tbsp butter
1 bottle (approx) red wine

Soak the prunes overnight to plump them. Soaking in cold tea gives them an excellent flavour. Cut the bacon into ½ inch cubes or small strips. Take a large heavy pot with a good lid. Heat about two tablespoons of butter in it and fry the bacon pieces until golden but not completely crisp. Transfer with a slotted spoon to a bowl then brown the onions in the same fat. Remove the onions to the same bowl and brown the mushrooms. When slightly brown remove and add to the bacon and onions. Now brown the rabbit pieces and season with a little salt and pepper as it browns. Add a little more butter if you have to, but the bacon should have given off enough fat. By now the juices at the bottom of the pan should be quite dark. Return the bacon, onions and mushrooms to the pan, add the bouquet garni and pour on enough wine to almost but not quite cover the meat. The quality of the wine is important; the more full bodied the better the dish. Season with not too much salt, because of the bacon. Bring to the boil and leave to simmer very, very gently. After 45 minutes add the prunes. Cook until the meat is really very tender, for at least another half an hour, perhaps more. Some of the prunes will break up and flavour the sauce. When the rabbit is tender, thicken the sauce. Mix two tablespoons of flour with an equal quantity of butter, drop teaspoons of this mixture into the simmering liquid, stirring a little. Do this a little at a time, just until the sauce reaches a velvety consistency. Cook for a further ten minutes after adding the flour before serving in a fondue or chafing dish with new potatoes and a french salad.

The beauty of this dish is that it tastes even better when reheated, so you can cook it the day before without a worry. A Burgundy or Beaujolais wine will give excellent results. Be sure to have another bottle to serve with the meal, for full enjoyment.

Ailsa Worthington

Venison Casserole

Leg venison (approx 2 lb meat)
2 oz butter (or 2 tablespoons oil)
Salt and pepper
½ lb streaky bacon
2 onions
3 level tablespoons plain flour

Marinade:

1 finely chopped onion
Sprig thyme
6 tbsp oil
½ pt red wine
1 clove crushed garlic
Bay leaf
2 tbsp brandy
½ pt stock

Marinade the meat minimum of 4 hours or overnight. Fry chopped bacon till fat runs. Add butter or oil and fry chopped onions and garlic. Add venison and brown. Add flour till brown. Add wine and enough stock to cover meat. Cook gently for ¾ - 1 hour then stir in strained marinade and continue cooking till meat is tender.

Catherine McCully
Kent

Venison Steaks with Duxelles and Prune Croûte

Serves 4

4 venison steaks
Salt and pepper
25 g (1 oz) butter
1 tbsp balsamic vinegar

For the marinade:

6 juniper berries
150 ml (¼ pt) red wine
3 tbsp olive oil
½ small onion, sliced
1 bay leaf

For the croûte:

1 small onion
4 - 6 dried prunes, stoned
1 tbsp lemon juice
4 slices bread, crusts removed
100 g (4 fl oz) flat mushrooms
25 g (1 oz) butter
1 garlic clove

1. Lightly crush the juniper berries and mix with the sliced onion and add the remaining marinade ingredients.
2. Place the steaks in a suitable dish and pour over the marinade, turn the steaks in the marinade a few times to coat well, cover and leave overnight.
3. Prepare croûtes, chop onion and the mushrooms very finely, chop the prunes and reserve. Heat the butter in a large pan and sauté the onions until soft, add the mushrooms and cook for 5 minutes. Season with salt and pepper, add lemon juice and prunes. Cook uncovered until all the liquid has evaporated and the mixture has formed a thick paste-like consistency.
4. Peel the garlic clove and slice in half and rub on the bread on both sides with the cut side of the garlic. Cut the bread into a neat shape and toast on both sides, spread the croûtes with the duxelles mixture and keep warm.
5. Remove the steaks from the marinade and pat dry. Heat butter in a frying pan and fry steaks over a high heat to brown all over. Reduce the heat slightly, add seasonings and cook steaks for 3 minutes on each side so that they are slightly pink.
6. Prepare sauce, strain marinade into a pan and bring to the boil and reduce by half. Remove steaks from pan and keep warm, deglaze pan with vinegar scraping up meat residue left from the steaks.

7. Add the reduced marinade and cook for two minutes.
8. Serve the steaks on the croûtes and pour sauce around on hot individual serving plates.

Eastbourne College of Food and Fashion
Rannies

Venison Goulash with Prunes, Bacon and a Crunchy Walnut Topping

Serves 4

2 tbsp olive oil
2 medium onions, sliced
2 tbsp flour
60 g pitted prunes (approx 12)
275 ml stock
600 g venison, casserole
1 tsp crushed garlic
250 ml red wine
3 rashers lean bacon, roughly chopped

Topping:

2 tsp marg
3 celery sticks
½ cup walnut pieces
Salt and pepper

Brown meat quickly in oil and remove. Lower heat and add onion and garlic. Add flour and cook for 1 minute then stir in red wine. Return meat to casserole and add prunes, bacon and stock. Season to taste. Cook until tender.

Before serving, make topping by quickly frying ingredients all together and spoon over casserole.

Heather Gow
Angus

Sliced Breast of Duck with Black Cherries

Serves 6

Six breasts of mallard duck
2 oz - 50 g butter
2 oz - 50 g black cherries
Freshly ground black pepper
4 tbsp walnut oil
¼ pt - 150 ml red wine
Freshly ground sea salt

The Sauce:

2 oz - 50 g butter
½ pt - 275 ml chicken stock
Freshly ground salt and pepper
2 oz - 50 g plain flour
6 oz - 175 g black cherries

Melt the butter in a saucepan. Take the saucepan away from the heat and stir in the flour. Cook the roux lightly until a golden brown then add the chicken stock flavoured with the black cherries. Season with salt and pepper. Cook the sauce through for about 5 minutes. Cover the sauce and leave on the side. This can be prepared well in advance.

Pre-heat the oven to gas 5 / 375°F / 190°C.

In a large sauté pan heat your oil then add your butter. When foaming add your well dried breasts of duck skin side down and cook gently for 8 minutes till nice and brown. Turn over and seal the fleshy underside for a few minutes. Transfer the duck breasts skin side up onto a rack over a roasting tin. Season with salt and pepper and pour on your red wine under the duck. Cover the duck lightly with tinfoil and cook in the oven for 30 minutes.

To Serve:

Heat up the sauce and add the red wine from under the duck and the cherries, simmer gently. Slice the duck breast thinly and arrange on a plate and spoon over the cherry sauce.

Mrs Beverley Parker
Kent

Chapter 7

Pasta

Pasta Carbonara

Serves 6

8 oz bacon (smoked if preferred)
5 oz milk, cream or crème fraîche
1 lb tagliatelle
3 eggs
Garlic (crushed)

Slice and fry bacon and garlic, whisk eggs and milk / cream, season it. Cook pasta with plenty of salt until al denté (approximately10 - 12 minutes). Drain it and return to the saucepan. Add cooked bacon to the egg mixture and pour over pasta, cook over low heat until liquid has been absorbed, check for seasoning.

Emma Donaldson
Pavia, Italy

Kew Gardens Asparagus and Almond Risotto

Serves 4

1 lb Arborio rice
2 - 3 shallots
2 oz nibbed almonds
1 - 1½ lb asparagus
3 - 4 pt stock
3 tbsp Parmesan cheese

Chop and soften shallots in little butter. Bring stock to boil. Add rice to shallots. Stir until coated - add stock until absorbed. Continue for 20 minutes until rice is soft, creamy and glutinous but with a bite. Cook asparagus. Fry almonds. Season rice and add cheese. Mix in asparagus and almonds.

Judy Patman
London

Tagliatelle Alla Cecca

Serves 4

12 oz tagliatelle
4 oz olive oil
4 oz chopped fresh basil leaves
5 large tomatoes
2 cloves of garlic
Salt and pepper

Drop tomatoes into boiling water for one full minute. Peel, seed and chop. Put into a large bowl with olive oil, garlic cloves sliced in two, basil leaves, salt and pepper. Let it stand for a couple of hours, then remove the garlic. Boil tagliatelle, drain and toss with the tomato mixture. Serve immediately.

Louise Melikoff
London

Pesto Pasta

1 bag of pasta quills (penne or wriggly)
Carton / jar fresh pesto sauce
Olive oil
Basil leaves
Jar of sundried tomatoes
Feta cheese

Cook the pasta for 10 minutes in large pan salted water. Meanwhile put pesto sauce in a bowl, add 4 tablespoons olive oil, 2 tablespoons white wine vinegar and whisk together. Drain pasta and rinse under cold tap until cool. Mix up with pesto mixture in a large dish then add sundried tomatoes (drained of their oil) and a good handful of olives and feta cheese chopped up into little cubes and scatter a few basil leaves on top.

Its delicious. All you need for lunch with some green salad. Even I can do it!

Fiona Gault
Kent

Lime Rice Tsarabajina

Serves 4

Into a big pan of boiling salted water throw 2 mugs of Basmati rice. Toss in 8 cardamoms and 2 vegetable stock cubes. Cook till done (when there is a tiny hard speck of white in the centre of a bitten grain of rice). Sieve and remove cardamoms. Steam or shake till dryish, then squeeze 4 ripe limes all over. Serve as an accompaniment to meat, fish or poultry. Being vegetarian, I like it on its own, topped with salted peanuts and a little soy sauce.

Joanna Lumley

Pasta Penne

Serves 4

200 g penne pasta
Garlic paste
1 tsp sugar
Chopped small onion
Salt and pepper
1½ lb best mince
3 tins Italian plum tomatoes
Tomato purée
Chopped carrots and courgettes
Olive oil
Bay leaf

Gently fry mince in olive oil till thoroughly sealed (10 - 15 minutes). Fry chopped onions in olive oil until golden. In large casserole, add drained tomatoes (reserve liquid), chopped vegetables, pepper, bay leaf, garlic, tomato purée and sugar. When meat is prepared, add to mixture and stir thoroughly adding reserved tomato liquid until covered. Cover with lid and cook slowly for at least two hours (until all ingredients thoroughly soft and cooked). Bring large pan of salted water to the boil and add pasta. Bring to boil and cook for 10 - 11 minutes (stir occasionally). Drain and stir in the meat sauce. Mix very well in large bowl and serve immediately.

Jacopo Astorino
Italy

Pasta with Boursin and Courgettes

Serves 4 - 5

2 lb courgettes
12 oz pasta twirls
8 oz Boursin cheese
Pepper
1½ onions (med)
2 oz butter
Parmesan cheese

Slice the onions into fine rings and the courgettes into thin slices at an angle. Cook both in melted butter until tender. Add to the pasta with lumps of Boursin cheese and sprinkle Parmesan on the top.

Mrs James Ogilvy
Scotland

Pasta Shells with Smoked Oysters and Quick Fried Spinach

Serves 4

12 oz small spinach leaves
8 - 10 oz pasta shells
3 large garlic cloves, chopped finely
Grated Parmesan to serve
2 x 3 oz cans smoked oysters / mussels
4 fl oz extra virgin olive oil
Salt and black pepper

Wash and dry spinach and chop finely. Cook pasta 7 - 12 minutes until al denté. Put olive oil in large, deep frying pan - high heat. Add garlic and spinach and stir swiftly, about 1 minute until spinach is limp. Stir in smoked oysters and oil. Season and mix with pasta. Serve immediately with Parmesan.

Rosemary Gow
Perth

Tagliatelle (Michael's favourite recipe)

Serves 4 (including 2 teenage boys!)

350 - 400 g pasta (preferably tagliatelle verdi)
1 lb bacon
Garlic to taste (2 - 3 cloves)
Approximately ¾ pt milk
4 eggs
Salt to taste
Ground black pepper

Chop bacon. Fry. Add crushed garlic to pan. Beat eggs. Add milk, salt and pepper. Meanwhile, cook pasta in boiling, salted water in a large pan. (It only takes about 5 minutes.) Add eggs and milk to bacon and garlic and heat slowly. Be careful not to overheat or eggs will scramble. When it begins to thicken, add the sauce to the cooked, drained pasta. Stir through. (The heat of the pasta will finish off cooking the sauce.) Serve with Parmesan cheese and a green side salad.

"And that's all for now, have a good evening!"

Michael Buerk
BBC Nine O' Clock News

My Pasta (Pasta Casa Nostra)

Serves 5 - 6

Olive oil
1 onion (optional)
1 lb tomatoes (or 2 tins)
1 green pepper
½ lb of mushrooms - if liked
2 or 3 cloves of garlic
Oregano - to taste
Black olives - to taste
½ red pepper - if you have one
Salt and freshly ground pepper
Dash of concentrated tomato paste and anything else you'd like it to taste of
Large packet of fresh pasta - my favourite is green tagliatelle

Into a pan of boiling salted water to which you've added a teaspoon of olive oil, drop in the pasta. About 5 minutes does it. Meanwhile add chopped garlic and onions to some olive oil in a pan. Add chopped tomatoes, the herbs and all, or some of the other ingredients. If you have half a glass of wine handy, add that too. Serve separately with plenty of freshly grated cheese.

Susannah York

Chilli non Carne

The best chilli you'll get this side of Tijuana! Serve with rice, mashed potatoes or avocado.

2 tbsp vegetable oil
1 medium onion, chopped
1½ level tsp chilli powder (or more according to taste)
2 x 4½ oz / 128 g packets TVP chunks or 4 vegetable burgers, crumbled
12 - 15 fl oz / 340 - 430 ml vegetable stock or water (6 fl oz if using vegetable burgers)
1 x 14 oz / 397 g tin chopped tomatoes
1 x 14 oz / 397 g tin red kidney beans
2 Mexican green chillies in brine, drained and chopped (optional)
Salt and freshly ground black pepper to taste

Heat the oil in a large saucepan and sauté the onion until golden brown. Add the chilli powder and TVP chunks and brown for 5 minutes. Add the vegetable stock and tomatoes, together with their juice. Cover the mixture and simmer for 20 minutes. Add the kidney beans and the chillies (if you are using them) and simmer for about 15 minutes, adding a little extra stock or water if necessary. Season to taste and serve hot.

45 minutes to cook
Good source of protein, vitamin A, vitamin C

Linda McCartney
Rye, East Sussex
Copyright Linda McCartney
MPL Communications Ltd

Vegetable Lasagne

2 oz butter / marg
Small head celery chopped
1¾ lb canned tomatoes in juice
1 tsp caster sugar
4 - 6 oz lasagne verde
8 oz onions peeled and sliced
8 oz mushrooms, sliced or quartered
1 bay leaf
Salt and fresh ground black pepper

Topping:

½ pt plain unsweetened yoghurt
Pinch cayenne pepper
2 tbsp rolled oats
3 oz Cheddar cheese grated
½ tsp mustard powder
Sliced tomatoes for garnish

1. Melt butter, soften onions and celery for 5 minutes.
2. Add mushroom, cook to absorb butter then add tomatoes and juice and bring to boil.
3. Add bay leaf, sugar, salt and pepper. Stir well, bring to boil and cook boiling rapidly for 20 minutes - stir to stop mixture sticking.
4. Pour half vegetable mix into base of 3 pint ovenproof dish. Cover well with lasagne. Repeat ending with lasagne layer.
5. Mix topping together except oats. Spread over lasagne. Sprinkle oats over the top.
6. Cook 180°C for 1 hour until golden. Garnish with sliced tomatoes. Serve with salad and fresh chunky bread.

Mrs John Martin
Kent

.... and now you've nearly cooked your way through this book, come and put your feet up in nourishing Normandy and let us cook for you (probably using these recipes!)

For a brochure and details contact Peter & Jenny Alliott

Château Des Rochers

50680 Cerisy-La-Forêt

Manche

France

Tel / fax: (010 33) 33 56 89 55

Chapter 8

Puddings

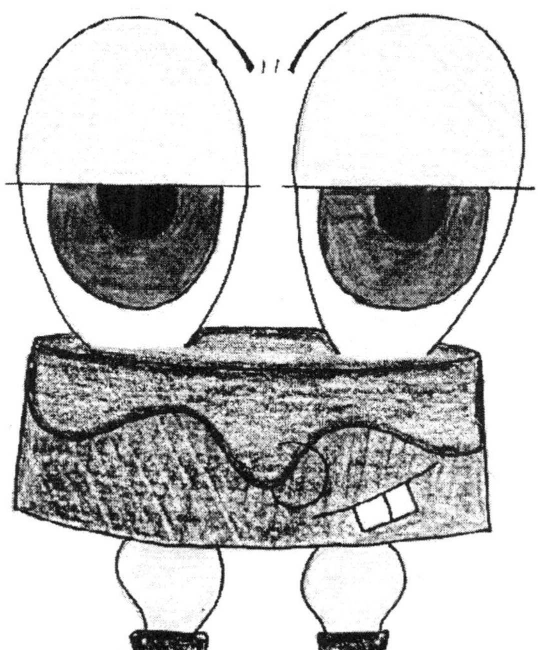

Apple and Mascarpone Cheese Delight

3 large Bramley apples
500 g (1 lb) blackberries
200 ml (8 fl oz) mascarpone cheese
Squeeze of lemon juice
100 g (4 oz) caster sugar
75 ml (3 fl oz) single cream

1. Quarter and core the Bramley apples. Place in a microwave dish, squeeze on the lemon juice and cover with microwave cling film, pierce several times. Microwave on full heat for six minutes. Sieve the Bramley mixture through a nylon sieve into a bowl, fork in the blackberries and leave to cool.
2. Whisk the mascarpone with your single cream and add to the purée, taste and add more sugar if needed. Chill well before serving.

Beverley Parker
Kent

Janey's Ice Cream

3 eggs (separated)
7 oz caster sugar
Juice and rind of 1 lemon
8 oz double cream

Beat the yolks, juice and rind together. Beat the whites and add sugar. Beat cream until thick and fold into yolk mixture with the whites. Put in container and freeze. Then add one of the following.

Blackcurrants - puréed with lemon juice
Banana - 3 puréed with half a lemon
Chocolate - reduce sugar to 5 oz and 1 oz cocoa
Coffee - 1tsp Nescafé in 1 oz warm water
Strawberry - 1 lb puréed + 5 oz sugar

Judy Patman
London

Mulberry Ice Cream (the easy way)

1 lb mulberries - washed
Squeeze of lemon juice
Sugar to taste
8 oz double cream

Put mulberries in food processor / liquidizer. Put through nylon sieve. Add sugar and lemon to taste. Whip cream and while whipping pour in mulberry syrup. Spoon into container and freeze.

Jennifer Dean
Kent

Iced Coffee Soufflés

Serves 6 - 8

4 eggs
2 tbsp powdered coffee
2 tbsp rum
Grated chocolate for decoration
¼ lb sugar
2 tbsp water
½ pint cream

Separate eggs and beat yolks with sugar and powdered coffee until mixture is thick and creamy. Melt chocolate and water in a small saucepan; add rum and stir into egg and coffee mixture. Whip cream and fold into soufflé mixture. Whisk egg whites and fold into mixture. Pour into individual soufflé dishes or custard cups and freeze for 4 hours. Decorate with grated chocolate.

Mrs Victor Pope
Kent

Summer Fruit Sabayon

2 egg yolks
Grated rind ½ lemon
4 tbsp cream / fromage frais
50 g (2 oz) caster sugar
150 ml (¼ pt) white wine
450 g (1 lb) mixed summer fruits

Beat the egg yolks and sugar in a bowl over a saucepan of boiling water, until it is well combined. Add lemon rind and wine, beat until smooth and thickened. Gradually stir in the cream and whisk for 1 minute until it is well combined. Arrange fruit in an ovenproof plate or bowl. Pour over the sabayon and place under a hot grill until bubbling and golden. Serve at once.

Eastbourne College of Food and Fashion
'Rannies'

Chocolate Mousse

3 egg yolks
4 tbsp water
½ pt double cream
2 oz sugar
6 oz (200 g) bar plain chocolate

Boil sugar and water. Break up chocolate in blender. Pour on hot syrup and blend on high speed. Add egg yolks and switch on for a few seconds. Lightly whip double cream and fold in chocolate mixture. Put in plastic box and freeze. Thaw to suit.

Phillada Pym
Kent

Brandysnap Cream

Very rich, very easy and very good

4 boxes brandysnaps (36 small snaps)
3 egg whites
1 pt double cream (600 ml)
1 tbsp brandy

1. Crush the brandysnaps (easiest in a Magimix).
2. Whip the cream lightly and fold in the crushed brandysnaps and the brandy.
3. Beat the egg whites into soft peaks and fold into the mixture.
4. Serve in individual dishes and chill for at least 6 hours.

Mrs Peter Stevens
Kent

Grand Marnier Parfait with Mango Purée

2 egg yolks
½ pt double cream
2 mangoes or one tin strained
2 oz caster sugar
2 tbsp Grand Marnier
Juice of half a lemon

Whisk the egg yolks with the sugar until pale and fluffy. Whip the cream until stiff and fold it with the Grand Marnier, into the egg yolk and sugar mixture. Pour into individual ramekins lined with foil and freeze for about two hours or until firm, but not solid. Peel and thinly slice the mangoes, reserving eight slices for garnishing. Purée the rest adding the lemon juice to sharpen the taste, (or purée strained fruit from a tin of mango slices).

To serve:

Turn out the parfaits on to individual serving plates surrounded with mango purée and decorate with mango slices.

Mrs Sally Lewers
Derbyshire

Butterscotch Walnut Pudding

Make sponge pudding mixture with pale muscovado sugar and add 3oz chopped walnuts, one teaspoon ground cinnamon, two tablespoons Camp coffee.

For butterscotch topping:

Put into pan 4 oz muscovado sugar, 2½ oz butter, 4 tablespoons cream. Place over gentle heat till melted, then boil for three minutes and pour into well greased basin. Steam for 1½ hours.

Mrs Reg Older
Kent

Ginger Ice Cream

Easy, quick and sophisticated. Serve with fruit

½ pt double cream
Jar of ginger conserve
1 tsp lemon juice
2 oz icing sugar
1 tsp yoghurt
4 eggs separated

Mix together egg yolks, icing sugar, ginger conserve, yoghurt, lemon juice. Whip cream and add to mixture folding in. Whip egg whites also folding in. Freeze.

Anne Crossley
Norfolk

Iced Christmas Pudding

¼ pt milk
1 tsp cocoa powder
2 oz raisins
1 oz currants
2 oz glacé cherries
½ pt thick cream
4 oz marshmallows
1 tsp instant coffee
1 oz sultanas
2 tbsp sherry (brandy or Kirsch)
2 oz blanched almonds

Put milk, marshmallows, coffee and cocoa in a saucepan. Heat gently, stirring occasionally, until the marshmallows are nearly melted. Allow to cool. Mix the dried fruit with the sherry. Allow to stand for 30 minutes then add to the marshmallow mixture with the quartered cherries and chopped nuts. Freeze the mixture for a short time until slightly thickened. Fold in the whipped cream and pack into a chilled basin. Freeze until firm. Turn out and decorate with cherries if liked, and serve with whipped cream or brandy butter and crisp biscuits. This can be made well in advance and stored in the freezer.

Lis Burroughs
Sussex

Strawberry Meringue Birthday Surprise

8 oz strawberries (puréed) and approx 6 strawberries for decoration
6 egg whites - weighed
Caster sugar (same weight as egg whites)
Granulated sugar (same weight as egg whites)
3 eggs
6 oz caster sugar
½ oz gelatine
2 egg yolks
1 pt double cream
Pinch of salt
Juice of ½ lemon - made up to 2½ fl oz with water
Cake tins same size as meringue circles

Whisk egg whites and salt until so stiff that the bowl can be held safely upside down. Whisk in caster sugar, a heaped tablespoon at a time. Fold in granulated sugar, a heaped tablespoon at a time. Make three circles of meringue on non-stick paper on oven trays - smoothing them to approximately half an inch thick and 7 inches across. Cook at 275°F / gas 1 for approximately one hour. Peel off paper and cool. Either mix egg yolks and sugar in a processor or whisk over hot water, until thick and mousse like. Half whip half of the cream. Dissolve gelatine in lemon juice over very gentle heat. Add purée, gelatine and cream to mousse. Pour into 2 foil lined cake tins, bringing foil over the top. Freeze. Remove from freezer and unwrap when frozen. Whip half a pint of cream. Cover one meringue circle with cream, place a strawberry circle on top, cover with cream, add meringue circle, cover with cream, add strawberry circle, cover with cream and top with the last meringue circle. Decorate with blobs of cream to support strawberries. With added candle holders and candles, it makes a marvellous "non cake" birthday cake. It should be assembled not earlier than the night before a dinner party and not later than three hours before serving. Should be kept in the fridge unless assembling on the day to be used.

Jane Reddish
London

Burnt Almond Cream

Custard:

4 egg yolks
¼ pt double cream
1 pt milk
4 oz caster sugar

Caramel:

2 oz granulated sugar
½ oz gelatine
1 tbsp water
¼ pt double cream
3 oz almonds (flaked)
1 tbsp Kirsch

Bring milk to boiling point. Beat egg yolks and pour on hot milk beating all the time. Return to pan and keep stirring until it thickens. Remove from heat and beat in sugar and cream. Leave on one side. Brown the almonds in oven and set aside. Make caramel by dissolving granulated sugar in the water until mixture turns a rich brown. Add cream and boil again. Add the dissolved gelatine (dissolved with 1 dstsp water). Stir caramel mixture into custard and when cold add the toasted almonds and Kirsch. Serve really cold.

Mrs Jenifer Dean
Kent

Blackcurrant Ice Cream

This ice cream is very quick, very simple and quite delicious. It needs no extra whippings in the course of freezing and it feeds 12. There is plenty for two lots of 6.

1 lb blackcurrants, fresh or frozen
3 tbsp crème de cassis
½ pt milk
½ lb sugar
½ pt double cream

Simmer the blackcurrants with the sugar and cassis until soft (after about 10 minutes), then mash them and push through a sieve. Whip the cream and milk together until thick and gradually add the cooked, sieved blackcurrant purée. Freeze in any suitable container and allow a quarter of an hour in the fridge before serving with a little more cassis.

Angela Parish
Kent

Cherry or Blackberry Cheesecake

8 oz digestive biscuits
1 lb Philadelphia cheese
3 small eggs
1 carton soured cream
2 - 3 drops vanilla essence
Pinch cinnamon
2 oz butter
6 oz sugar
6 - 8 drops almond essence
1 tbsp sugar
Pinch nutmeg
Cherry pie filling (1 or 2 cans) or bramble jelly and shredded coconut

1. Crush biscuits and melt butter. Add cinnamon. Grease a 9 inch flan dish and line with biscuit mixture and pat flat. Freeze for 10 - 15 minutes.
2. In mixer or by hand, cream the cheese and add sugar. Then add eggs and beat until thick and creamy (2 minutes). Add almond essence. Pour into flan case, and bake at gas 5 for 20 - 25 minutes. Leave to cool for 10 minutes.
3. Mix soured cream in with sugar. Add vanilla. Pour over cheesecake and bake for 5 minutes, gas 5.
4. When baked, sprinkle with nutmeg and leave to cool. (Can be frozen at this time if desired.)

5. Chill completely. To serve, top with two cans of cherry pie filling or bramble jelly with some nutmeg or coconut.

Roufina Hunn
Kent

Chocolate Cream Pudding

4 oz marshmallows
2 oz cooking chocolate
¼ pt whipped double cream
10 fl oz milk
2 tsp instant coffee
2 tbsp sherry (more if desired)
2 oz each chopped dried apricots, cherries, raisins, nuts

Put milk, marshmallows, coffee and chocolate in saucepan and heat gently until melted and blended. Mix dried fruit with sherry and allow to marinate for half an hour, then add to marshmallow mixture and add nuts and cherries. Freeze for a short time until slightly thickened. Fold in whipped cream. Place in basin lined with cling film and freeze. Turn out onto a dish / plate and put in the fridge until required - about 1 hour. Decorate and serve.

Jean Thompson
Kent

Real Bread Pudding

1 loaf stale bread
3 oz marg / butter
2 oz sultanas
1 dozen glacé cherries
2 - 3 tbsp mixed spice
Water for soaking
4 oz raisins
2 oz currants
2 - 3 tsp granulated sugar
Granulated sugar for top

Thoroughly soak loaf in water. Squeeze out excess water and place in large mixing bowl. Add margarine and work in the bread using hands. Then add the rest of ingredients except topping sugar. Mix well after using hands. Put in a well greased ovenproof dish. Sprinkle sugar on top. Bake in oven at 170°C for about 45 minutes.

Cherylynn Lang
Kent

Treacle Tart with a difference

12 oz short crust pastry

Filling:

6 tbsp golden syrup
4 tbsp milk
3 oz fresh white breadcrumbs
2 oz butter
2 beaten eggs
Finely grated rind and juice 2 lemons

Line an 11 inch loose bottomed flan dish with pastry. Warm the golden syrup and butter in a bowl over hot water and when the butter has melted, remove from the heat and add milk, rind and juice of lemons and the beaten eggs. Mix thoroughly then stir in the breadcrumbs. At this point you can add sultanas and / or peel. Pour into the pastry shell and bake at 375°F for 25 - 30 minutes. Serve hot. This is a delicious treacle tart, much lighter than the traditional one and will not pull your teeth out!

Sarah Gracey
Kent

New Zealand Pavlova

Serves 8

3 egg whites
1 teaspoon lemon juice
Fruit
6 oz caster sugar
½ pt double cream

Turn the oven on to 240°C (very hot). Cut a circle of baking parchment slightly larger than a 10 inch pyrex or ovenproof plate and place it on the plate. Beat the egg whites very stiff. Add the sugar and lemon juice all together, beat again until very shiny. Spread on paper on the plate. Put it in the oven and turn the oven off. Leave until cold. Place serving plate face down on meringue. Turn it all over. Remove pyrex plate and peel off baking parchment. Whip cream stiffly and spread on pavlova. Decorate with raspberries or fruit of your choice.

Phillada Pym
Kent

Very Easy Rich Chocolate Ice Cream

300 g dark chocolate
1 tin condensed milk
1 pt double cream or whipping cream

Melt chocolate with a little cream. When melted, cool, blend remaining cream and condensed milk. Pour into ramekins and freeze. When serving, decorate with cream, chocolate or Baileys Irish Cream. Could add brandy to mixture.

Amanda Gow
Kent

Black Cherry Surprise

Serves 6

3 tins stoned black cherries (drained)
1 pt double cream
Demerara sugar for sprinkling
1 tub (450 g) low fat natural yoghurt
3 tbsp cherry liqueur

Place drained cherries into dish. Add cherry liqueur. Whisk cream until thick and fold in yoghurt. Pour over cherries. Sprinkle sugar over cream mixture and chill in fridge. (The brown sugar will melt and make an attractive topping.)

Maria Sevens
Kent

Quick Vanilla Ice Cream

½ pt milk
14 oz Nestlé condensed milk
½ pt cream (whipping)
1½ tsp real vanilla essence

Mix all ingredients in a jug and pour into ice cream maker. Add fudge bits or choc chips if desired. Delicious served with hot fudge sauce.

Jill Robinson
Northants

Chestnut and Chocolate Mousse

4 oz plain chopped chocolate
½ pt milk
2 eggs, separated
2 oz soft light brown sugar
Can unsweetened chestnut purée
½ pt whipped cream
½ oz gelatine, soaked in 3 tbsp cold water

Gently heat the chocolate in a small pan with milk until melted. Beat egg yolks and sugar together until creamy, then stir in the chocolate mixture. Return to the pan and heat gently, stirring until thickened. Stir in gelatine. Beat chestnut purée with a little of mixture until smooth, then mix in the remainder. Cool. Fold in two thirds of cream. Whisk the egg whites until stiff and fold in. Turn into a lightly oiled cake tin (7 inch) and chill until set. Turn out onto a plate. Decorate with remaining cream.

Mrs Stephen Saunders
Kent

Rhubarb Meringue Torte

Base:

1 (7½ oz) packet gingernuts
2 level tbsp golden syrup
2 oz butter

Filling:

1½ lb rhubarb
6 oz caster sugar
¼ pint water
2 level tbsp cornflour
2 eggs

Grease a deep, round, loose-bottomed 8½ inch cake tin. Place biscuits between greaseproof paper and crush with a rolling pin. Carefully measure syrup and place in a saucepan. Add butter and heat until melted. Remove from heat and stir in crushed biscuits. Press mixture on base of cake tin. Wash and trim rhubarb, cut into short lengths. Place 3 oz caster sugar and water in a saucepan, add rhubarb and simmer gently until just tender. Drain rhubarb, reserving syrup. Blend cornflour with a little water in a pan. Stir in rhubarb syrup, bring to the boil, stirring, and cook for 2 minutes. Remove from heat. Separate eggs and place whites in a clean bowl. Add yolks to saucepan, mix well. Carefully stir in rhubarb, then spread mixture in tin. Prepare a medium grill. Whisk egg whites until stiff. Whisk in half the remaining sugar, then fold in the remainder using a metal spoon. Pile meringue on top of rhubarb mixture. Place under grill for several minutes until golden brown. Cool. Loosen from tin and slide onto serving dish.

Caroline Philipson
Kent

Oranges in Caramel

6 oranges
¼ pt warm water
¼ pt cold water
8 oz granulated sugar

Prepare caramel by dissolving the sugar in the cold water over a low heat. When the sugar is completely dissolved bring to the boil and cook until it is light brown. To stop overcooking, hold the base of the pan over a bowl of warm water, then, carefully add a quarter of a pint of warm water to the caramel mixture (which may spit as you add the water) and reheat it gently to dissolve the caramel again. Leave to cool. Slice the oranges, either removing the peel and pith and slicing across, or by peeling and slicing the segments clear of the pith. Put into a dish and pour over the caramel.

Mrs Richard Boddington
Somerset

The Very Best Crumble Topping

9 oz plain flour
3 oz ground almonds
3 oz demerara sugar
4½ oz softened butter
2 oz flaked almonds

1. Rub butter into flour and stir in the rest of the ingredients.
2. Sprinkle over any cooked fruit mixture (blackberry and apple is nice).
3. Cook for 30 - 40 minutes at 180°C.
4. Serve hot or cold with custard, cream, greek yoghurt or crême fraîche.

Sue Maudling
Kent

Hot Buttered Plums Baked in Bread

This is a really delicious pudding quick to assemble and very financially reasonable.

Serves 4 usually

Allow two plums per person
8 ripe black plums
Approx 8 slices white bread, about ½ inch thick
Butter, (enough to spread the bread generously)
8 tablespoons sugar
Cream for serving and a little Prunelle or plum brandy or ordinary brandy

Butter the bread generously, remove the crusts. Halve and stone the plums. Preheat oven 200°C / gas 6 / 400°F. Push the plum halves onto the buttered bread, skin side down. Lay in a shallow baking dish and sprinkle lightly with the sugar. Put a dob of butter onto plum halves and bake for approximately 20 minutes till plums are bubbly and bread is brown and crispy. Serve very hot sprinkling each plum with a touch of brandy. Serve with any type of cream.

Anne Neame
Kent

Malakoff Gateau

Serves 8

2 packets of sponge fingers
4½ oz caster sugar
¼ pt single cream
½ - ¾ pt strong black coffee
4½ oz butter
2 egg yolks
6 oz ground almonds

To serve:

Amaretto
½ pint whipping or double cream
Toasted almonds to sprinkle over the top

Cream the butter and sugar together until fluffy. Add the egg yolks, ground almonds and single cream to the above. Brush a loaf tin lightly with oil. Dip the sponge fingers one by one into the coffee carefully (if you leave them too long they go soggy). Line the bottom of the tin with sponge fingers as you finish dipping each one. Spread a layer of the almond mixture on top of the sponge fingers and then repeat with more sponge fingers and another layer of almond mixture. Finish with a layer of coffee-dipped sponge fingers and then refrigerate. I found it easier to freeze at this point - it freezes very well. Turn out of tin and decorate with whipped cream and Amaretto poured over. Sprinkle the toasted almonds over the top of the gateau.

Judith Findon
Lincolnshire

Mascarpone Ice Cream

Makes 1½ litres

¼ pint milk
1 rounded tsp cornflour
500 g mascarpone cheese
4 egg yolks
6 oz caster sugar
500 g fromage frais

Make a usual custard with the first four ingredient, then whip in the cheese and fromage frais. Freeze for 2 hours, whip again. Do that twice. Leave in the fridge for one hour before serving. This is very good with a fruit compôte, or anything that's a bit sweet.

Mrs James Varley
Herefordshire

Pineapple Surprise

7 oz pineapple (tin)
5 oz cream
4 oz marshmallows (small)

Crush pineapple, soak with marshmallows overnight. Whisk cream and add to pineapple and marshmallows. Cool and serve.

Penny Donaldson
Devon

White Chocolate Mousse

125 g white chocolate
¼ cup caster sugar
2 cups cream
½ cup liqueur
1 tsp vanilla essence
2 tbsp grated chocolate

Heat chocolate over hot water or in microwave at medium heat. Add half the liqueur and all the sugar. Stir until smooth. Cool. Whip cream and the rest of the liqueur. Fold chocolate mixture and grated chocolate into whipped cream. Spoon into small individual dishes or into a serving dish - delicious. Freezes well.

This is a New Zealand recipe which is wonderful to make in Brussels where white chocolate is such a special food of Belgium.

Janet Taylor
New Zealand and Brussels

Quick Pudding

Left over fruit salad
Small tin condensed milk
Left over cream

Put condensed milk, in the tin, in a saucepan of boiling water for 1 hour. When cool, mix with cream and fruit salad in Magimix and put in freezer. Eat with fresh raspberries.

Mrs Richard Henderson
Kent

Raspberry and Cinnamon Torte

Serves 6

5 oz soft margarine
5 oz ground almonds
1 egg
1 lb raspberries (fresh or frozen)
Double cream
5 oz caster sugar
5 oz self raising flour
Ground cinnamon
Icing sugar
Greek yoghurt

1. Place margarine and caster sugar, almonds, flour and egg in a bowl with 1 level teaspoon of ground cinnamon, beat well.
2. Grease and base line an 8½ inch loose bottomed cake tin.
3. Spread half the almond mixture into the tin using a fork or spatula to flatten slightly. Sprinkle over the raspberries, then dot over the remaining almond mixture so that it covers the fruit.
4. Stand the tin on a baking sheet and bake at 180°C / 350°F / gas 4 for about 1 hour, covering lightly when well browned. The torte should feel just firm to the touch with a springy texture. Cool in the tin for about 1 hour.
5. Dust with mixed cinnamon and icing sugar and serve warm accompanied by lightly whipped cream, folded through with Greek yoghurt.

Not suitable for freezing.

Sarah Kerr
Avon

Tessa's Rhubarb Princess of Puddings

1½ lb rhubarb
3 oz butter
Grated rind and juice of 1 lemon
5 eggs separated
½ pint milk
3 oz soft brown sugar
8 oz caster sugar
Grated rind and juice of 2 oranges
2 oz flour

Wash and cut the rhubarb into bite-sized pieces. Cook for 10 minutes with the soft brown sugar, till just soft but firm. Beat butter and add caster sugar. Beat in rinds and then juice. Beat in five yolks, one by one. Sieve the flour and beat in and lastly add milk. Whisk egg whites until stiff and fold in. Pour mixture over the rhubarb and bake in a bain-marie for 40 minutes, or until golden brown. Watch it for burning and cook at 160°C or bottom of top Aga oven, gas 3. Serve with crème fraîche.

Mary Spry
Kent

Primrose's Minty Choc Bombe

Meringues:

4 egg whites
4 oz granulated sugar
4 oz caster sugar

Make meringues by whipping egg whites until stiff and dry. Add caster sugar gradually and fold in the granulated sugar and beat until stiff. Drop spoonfuls onto non stick paper and bake it in very slow oven, (200° F) until firm and crisp. This may take about four to five hours.

Bombe:

1 pint whipping cream
12 After Eight or similar mints
2 liqueur glasses Crème de Menthe

Lightly whip cream. Sweeten to taste with icing sugar. Break meringues into three or four pieces and fold into cream with crème de menthe and mints broken into little bits. Freeze, (I use a plastic bowl with a lid). Take out and decorate with chocolate pieces. This can be served straight from the freezer as it never gets too hard.

Mrs Ralph Reynolds
Hants

Chilled Martian Mousse

Serves 3 or 4

3 large Mars bars
½ pt (250 - 300 ml) double cream
1 tablespoon (14 ml) milk
1 egg white

To decorate:

Milk flake or chocolate curls

To serve:

Whipped cream and meringues (optional)

Thinly slice the Mars bars and put in a bowl with the milk over a pan of simmering water until smooth. Stir occasionally and make sure all lumps are gone but don't let it harden. Whisk the cream until just stiff and using a metal spoon fold it into the caramel mixture. Whisk the egg white and fold it in making sure everything is well mixed. Put in a freezer-safe dish, cover and freeze for at least three hours. Take out before the meal and decorate with milk flake or chocolate curls and serve with whipped cream and meringues (optional).

Mrs Michael Oppeeman
Worcestershire

Bananas and Cream

Serves 4

Bananas, 1 per person
4 oz sugar
Juice of 1 lemon
Cream and grated chocolate

Slice bananas into individual bowls. Gently dissolve sugar in lemon juice, then bring to the boil and leave without stirring until the juice becomes thick and syrupy. Pour over bananas, add a spoonful of thick cream (see note below) and garnish with grated chocolate.

A Note on Crème Cru

Crème cru is wonderful thick natural cream, served from large stone jars in the markets and in most supermarkets in France. It has a very rich taste almost as though flavoured with lemon, but not like soured cream. It can be boiled in sauces and added to pan juices, (with the addition of mustard and brandy or white wine) and can be used on its own or as an accompaniment to any fish or meat. It lasts a long time in the fridge and is equally delicious with any fruit or sweet dishes.

Crème fraîche is also delicious but has not quite the same rich favour in my opinion. If I was on a day trip to France, I would put crème cru on the top of my shopping list!

Mrs Jenny Alliott
Normandy

Pecan Pie Ice Cream

10 fl oz milk
4 egg yolks
½ pt whipping or double cream
3 oz pecans
Vanilla essence
4 oz soft brown sugar
12 oz left-over pecan pie

Warm milk gently. Whisk egg yolks and sugar then pour milk in, stirring all the time. Pour this back into saucepan stirring until it forms a coating custard. Leave to cool then fold in stiffly whipped cream. Break the pecan pie into bite sized pieces and fold them and the additional pecans into the ice cream. Freeze. When it is beginning to freeze to the sides of the bowl, turn it out and stir. Then replace it into a ring mould and leave to freeze solid. Remove from the freezer and refrigerate it 1 hour before serving.

You could make meringues with the egg whites to serve with the ice cream.

Annabel Mowll
Kent

Brandy Mousse Ice Cream

Whites of 2 size one eggs
6 tbsp water
3 - 5 tbsp brandy
Good pinch salt
6 oz demerara sugar
1 tsp vanilla essence
¾ pt whipping cream

For caramelized almond top:

1 oz caster sugar
2 oz flaked almonds

Whisk the egg whites with the salt until they form soft peaks. Dissolve the demerara with the water in a saucepan, stirring over a low heat. Then increase the heat and boil fiercely without stirring for three minutes. Pour immediately onto egg whites in a thin stream whisking all the time with an electric whisk at high speed. Gradually whisk in vanilla essence and brandy. Continue whisking until the mixture is fairly thick. In a separate bowl whisk the cream until thick but not stiff and gently fold into the egg white mixture with a metal spoon. Freeze for at least five hours. This ice cream can come straight from the freezer to the table!

For the topping: mix the caster sugar with the flaked almonds. Heat an ungreased frying pan and tip in mixture, stirring all the time. When caramelized, tip out and separate the almonds as they cool. Sprinkle on ice cream.

Sara Hurst
London

Apricot, Apple Toffee Upside-Down Pudding

Serves 6

Oven 190°C / 375°F / gas 5

Topping:

4 oz (110 g) dried apricots
4 oz (110 g) butter
8 oz (225 g) cooking apples
4 oz (110 g) brown sugar

Pudding:

6 oz (175 g) self raising flour
3 oz (75 g) butter
2 eggs, size 2
1 tsp vanilla essence
¼ tsp salt
3 oz (75 g) caster sugar
3 tbsp cold milk

Make topping first. Soak apricots in boiling water for 20 minutes. Drain well and add to thinly sliced apples. In a saucepan melt butter and sugar together until they are completely blended. Then pour into the bottom of a 2 pint ovenproof dish. Arrange the apples and apricots on top of this. To make the pudding, put all of the ingredients except the milk, eggs and the vanilla essence into a food processor. Switch on and process until mixture resembles fine breadcrumbs, then add milk, eggs and vanilla essence to form a batter. Spread this evenly on top of the apples and apricots. Bake in centre of preheated oven for 30 minutes 190°C / 375°F / gas 5. Reduce the temperature to 180°C / 350°F / gas 4 and bake for a further 15 minutes or until the pudding feels firm. Leave for 5 minutes in dish, then loosen edges by sliding a knife around sides of the dish. Then turn upside - down onto serving dish. Delicious with fromage frais.

Diana Tosswill
London

Raspberry and Banana Fool

Serves 6

½ lb raspberries (fresh or frozen)
Juice ½ lemon and ½ orange
½ pt double cream
3 large ripe bananas
4 oz sugar

Peel and roughly chop the bananas. Process bananas until reduced to a purée. Add raspberries, lemon and orange juice and sugar and process to a smooth purée. Whip cream until thick and gradually mix into fruit purée. Turn into bowl and chill well.

This is a delicious and very simple pudding. Enjoyed by one and all of all ages!

Mrs Charlie Simkins
Kent

Toffee and Banana Crumble

Serves 4

200 g (7 oz) tin condensed milk
100 g (4 oz) unsalted butter
3 bananas
250 g (8 oz) plain flour
100 g (4 oz) caster sugar

To make the toffee:

Place the un-opened tin of condensed milk in the pan of water and boil for 3 hours, topping up the boiling water as necessary. Leave the tin to cool. Pre-heat the oven to 180°C / 350°F / gas 4 and grease an ovenproof dish.

To make the crumble:

Rub the flour and the butter together until the mix is like fine crumbs, then add the sugar. Chop the bananas and spoon into the dish, top with the toffee and sprinkle over the crumble. Bake in the oven for about 15 - 20 minutes until the crumble is golden brown.

Alison Cahill
Essex

Lime and Grape Mousse

Serves 6 - 8

5 limes
4 large eggs, separated
4 oz caster sugar
8 oz black or green grapes
1 sachet gelatine - approximately ½ oz
½ pint double cream

Grate the rind of the limes into a bowl. Add the egg yolks. Squeeze the juice from the limes into a small saucepan and sprinkle the gelatine over. Heat gently until the gelatine granules dissolve, then raise the temperature until the lime juices are very hot, but not actually boiling. Meanwhile, whisk the egg yolks and rind, gradually incorporating the caster sugar, until the mixture is very thick and pale. Still whisking, add the very hot lime juice and gelatine mixture in a stream (not too fast, rather like adding oil to mayonnaise). Whisk in well and leave the mixture until it is very thick. Whip the cream and fold it in. Whisk the egg whites until very stiff and using a large metal spoon, fold them quickly and thoroughly into the mousse, along with the grapes which have been halved and seeded. Pour into a glass or china serving dish and leave in a cool place. If you like, top with more whipped cream and more halved grapes.

Mrs Vyvyan Harmsworth
Kent

Cheesecake

1 lb (approx) Philadelphia cream cheese
1 large egg
½ tsp vanilla essence
3 oz butter
5 oz caster sugar
6 oz digestive biscuits crushed
Double or whipped cream

Melt butter, mix into crushed biscuits. Line a 9 inch flan tin with mixture then put it in the fridge for half an hour. Mix cream cheese, egg, caster sugar and vanilla essence in Magimix. Pour into flan dish and put in a very cool oven for half an hour. Allow to cool overnight in a fridge and top with whipped cream.

Jilly Cunningham
Sussex

Tarte Tatin

3 - 3½ lb apples, (Granny Smiths are best)
4 oz butter (unsalted is best)
7 oz sugar
8 oz short crust pastry (frozen)

Preheat oven to 425°F / 220°C. Melt butter in a large frying pan over medium heat. Peel the apples, cut into 4 or 8 depending on size and add them with the sugar. Cook for about 15 minutes, turning occasionally, but trying not to break up the apples too much. Raise heat and continue in the same manner allowing mixture to brown quite a lot. The liquid evaporates and becomes almost caramelized. Tip mixture into a Tarte Tatin tin. Roll out pastry to fit top of tin, tucking edges in loosely. Bake for 20 minutes, until the pastry is cooked and invert onto a heat-proof plate. Allow to cool a little before serving or it can be gently heated if cooked in advance. Serve with lots of whipped cream (or ice-cream).

A Tarte Tatin tin is about 8 inches in diameter and 2 inches deep. I don't have a non-stick one and just butter it lightly, but you can get non-stick ones which don't need greasing.

Mrs Ben Hay
Kent

Bistro Cheesecake

Very simple and quick to make, delicious and freezes well

Base:

¼ lb digestive biscuits
1 oz caster sugar
1½ oz unsalted butter

Melt butter, add crushed biscuits and sugar. Line flan tin.

Filling:

Small tin full fat condensed milk
4 oz Philadelphia cheese
2 lemons

Mix milk and cheese in a liquidiser or mixer. Pour in juice of lemons and if desired grated rind of 1 lemon (mix quickly to avoid curdling). Pour into base immediately and decorate. This will fill a 7 inch flan dish.

Di Brown
Kent

Chocolate Amaretti Pudding

Serves 12

12 oz chocolate
2 x 300 g boxes Amaretti biscuits
6 tbsp cider
1½ pt double cream
8 tbsp brandy
Grated chocolate for decoration
Double cream for serving
3 pt pudding basin (lined with cling film - optional)

1. Line pudding basin with cling film.
2. Break up chocolate into a heatproof bowl over a saucepan of barely simmering water and leave until melted.
3. Heat cream in another saucepan to just below boiling.
4. Pour hot cream into electric mixer bowl and add melted chocolate.
5. Whisk to blend for a few seconds.
6. Stand mixer bowl in a basin / sink of cold water until cold.
7. Whisk until a thick chocolate cream.
8. Mix brandy and cider in bowl.
9. Spread a layer of chocolate cream onto the base of the pudding bowl (lined with cling film).
10. Dip Amaretti biscuits, a few at a time, into the brandy and cider, then into the chocolate cream and arrange a layer of 4 or 5 in the base of the pudding bowl.
11. Spread a layer of chocolate cream over the biscuits.
12. Continue, repeating 10 and 11.
13. Leave overnight in fridge.
14. Turn the pudding out onto serving dish and serve with cream.

Mrs John Barton
Kent

Boodles Fool

Serves 12

2 packets (16 squares) sponge cake
Juice of 3 lemons
4 - 6 oz sugar
Juice 6 oranges
1 pt single cream
¼ - ½ pt double or whipping cream

Break the sponge cakes into a large, shallow serving dish. Mix the orange and lemon juice and stir in the single cream. Add enough sugar to make the mixture just sweet, (remember the sponge cakes have quite a sweet crust) and pour this over the sponge so that all pieces become slightly saturated. Chill for an hour or two, then decorate with the lightly whipped double or whipping cream.

Di McKenzie
Kent

Trifle - a family favourite

Sponge cake
1 oz blanched almonds cut into strips
Grated lemon rind
Tinned Devon custard
Crystallised fruit to decorate
4 macaroons
4 - 5 tablespoons sherry
Strawberry jam
Whipped cream

Put a layer of sponge cake in dish and cover with broken macaroons, almonds, lemon rind, sherry and a layer of strawberry jam. Pour over with custard, top with cream and decorate with the fruits.

Jackie Bishop
Kent

Baked Peaches

Serves 6

6 peaches (halved and stoned)
Butter
Demerara sugar
Cream or Mascarpone ice cream

Put halved peaches in lightly buttered baking dish. Put one teaspoon of sugar into centre of each peach half. Top with small portion of butter, cover with foil and bake in moderate oven for roughly 30 minutes or until soft. Serve hot or cold.

Mrs Ian Johnton
Kent

Magpie

Pastry:

8 oz plain flour
Water to mix
4 oz butter
Pinch salt

Make the shortcrust pastry and bake blind in a 9 inch fluted pie dish 190°C for 25 minutes. (Mould tin foil in pastry case for baking blind.) Reduce oven to 180°C.

Filling:

425 g tin apricots
4 oz ground almonds
A few flaked almonds
405 g tin condensed milk
1 beaten egg

Arrange apricots in bottom of pastry case. Mix condensed milk, ground almonds and beaten egg in a bowl. Pour this mixture over apricots in the flan case and top with a few flaked almonds. Bake for 35 - 40 minutes until filling is set. Serve hot or cold.

Mrs Tom Harris
Kent

Peaches and Brandy

Serves 2

4 peaches
4 tbsp brandy
4 tbsp caster sugar

Peel and quarter the peaches and add the caster sugar and the brandy to every four peaches. Serve with cream.

Mrs F Horne
Kent

Caramel Shortcake Tart

Cream 1 dessertspoon sugar and 3 oz butter. Add 1 egg unbeaten and lastly a small breakfast cup of flour and 1 teaspoon baking powder. Mix and press into buttered tin.

Make caramel in saucepan with:

1 tablespoon golden syrup
2 oz butter
2 egg yolks
A little vanilla
½ tin sweetened condensed milk
¾ cup brown sugar
2 tbsp flour, put in last

Melt altogether and boil very slowly for a few minutes, then pour into tart base. Lastly beat egg whites stiff with 4 tablespoons sugar and put on top of caramel. Bake in slow oven 300°F / 150°C for about an hour.

Mrs Robert MacCall
Kent

Favourite Chocolate Ice Cream

7 egg yolks
6 oz melted chocolate - plain
4 oz caster sugar
1 pint whipped cream

Beat the yolks and the sugar in a bowl until it is thick, stir in the melted chocolate and fold in the cream. Freeze it either in a loaf tin or in a ring mould. Decorate with whipped cream and some grated chocolate.

Lady Anthony Hamilton
Northern Ireland

Coffee Marshmallow Pudding

54 (250 g) marshmallows
6 tsp instant coffee dissolved in 1½ cups boiling water
1 pt double cream
Unsweetened chocolate and little biscuits to decorate

Melt marshmallows in double saucepan with coffee and water. After mixture is liquid, cool and put in fridge for 20 minutes. Whip up double cream and fold into cooled marshmallow mixture. Shave chocolate on top and decorate with biscuits.

Sally
Surrey

Lemon Dessert

Base:

8 oz digestive or ginger biscuits
2 tbsp sugar
4 oz margarine (melted)

Crush biscuits, add melted margarine and sugar and line dish.

Filling:

1 small tin condensed milk
Rind and juice of 2 lemons
1 small carton cream

Whip cream until stiff and add condensed milk. Stir in rind and juice of lemons - now thickens - pour into case and refrigerate.

Mrs D Piper
Kent

Lemon Mousse

Serves 4

2 lemons, juice and rind
4 eggs (free range)
6 oz caster sugar
Slightly under ½ oz gelatine (1 sachet)

Use an electric hand whisk if possible. Whisk yolks and sugar until light and fluffy. Grate lemon rind. Heat the lemon juice and gelatine over a VERY low heat until dissolved, let it cool down but not set. Beat the egg whites until they are stiff. Beat gelatine mixture into the eggs and sugar mixture then fold egg whites in with a metal spoon. Lastly, fold in the lemon rind, leave a little to decorate the top of the mousse. Put in the fridge or cool place.

Joanna David

Crème de Menthe Soufflé

1 sachet gelatine
8 oz caster sugar
½ pt whipped cream
Grated chocolate
4 egg yolks
4 tbsp crème de menthe
4 egg whites

Soak the gelatine in three tablespoons of cold water. Dissolve over a low heat in a pan of hot water. Add crème de menthe. Mix egg yolks and sugar together until light and fluffy. Add the gelatine in a steady stream. Whisk egg whites until peaking. Whip cream. Fold in egg whites and cream. Pour some mousse into a glass then put some grated chocolate on top. Continue in layers until the glass is full.

Steve Thorley
Catering Manager, Ashford School

Very Simple and Quick Banana Cream

Serves 4

3 ripe bananas
Juice of one lemon
4 oz sugar
½ pt double cream

Peel bananas and process until smooth. Put puréed bananas into a small saucepan with sugar and lemon juice and heat to boiling point, stirring to prevent sticking. Leave to cool. Whip the cream evenly and fold into banana mixture. Chill. Serve with brandysnaps.

Anonymous

Chapter 9

Cakes

Oven Soda Bread

16 oz soda bread flour

½ pt milk or buttermilk

Add milk to flour, mix quickly and lightly to a soft dough. Roll out one inch thick. Bake for 35 mins in a preheated oven, gas 6 / 400°F / 200°C or until ready. Cool on a wire rack.

Mrs Ann Radford
Northern Ireland

Blitzen Torte

1½ oz margarine
Pinch salt
¼ tsp vanilla essence
2 oz flour
2 egg whites
1 tsp caster sugar
5 oz caster sugar
2 egg yolks
1 tbsp milk
¼ tsp baking powder
2 oz almonds, blanched and sliced
1/8 tsp cinnamon

Filling:

4 oz plain cooking chocolate
1 egg yolk
1 tsp brandy (optional)
Cream
1 oz butter
1 tsp gelatine (optional)

Method:

1. Grease and line the bottoms of 2 sandwich tins.
2. Cream margarine and 2 oz sugar, add yolks, vanilla essence, milk and flour sifted with baking powder and spread mixture in the bottoms of the tins.
3. Whisk egg whites until light, add 3 oz caster sugar gradually and spread on unbaked mixture. Sprinkle with almonds, sugar and cinnamon.
4. Bake at 350°F for about 30 minutes.
5. Filling. Mix together chocolate, yolk, brandy and gelatine. Add butter and enough cream to make a smooth paste.
6. Sandwich the cakes with the filling when the cake is cool.

Di McKenzie
Kent

Parkin

1 cup margarine
1 cup plain flour
½ cup raisins or other dried fruit
½ tsp salt
2 eggs
1 cup soft brown sugar
1 cup porridge oats
4 tbsp golden syrup
½ tsp bicarbonate of soda

Melt margarine, sugar and syrup slowly in a large saucepan. Meanwhile sift together flour, salt and bicarbonate of soda. When sugar mixture has melted allow to cool, then stir in flour, salt and bicarbonate of soda. Whisk eggs and add with the dried fruit to the mixture. Give it all a good mix. It should be a wet mixture. Pour into a lined tin and bake at gas 5 / 375°F / 190°C. Leave for approximately 20 minutes. The sides should be firm and slightly shrunk from the side of the tin. If the centre is still soft it does not matter. Allow to cool in tin for a while then cut it into squares and lift out. This makes a squishy but nutty parkin which keeps fresh for a long time and freezes well.

Rosemary Raymond
Kent

Paradise Cake

4 oz margarine
1 egg
2 tbsp chopped glacé cherries
2 tbsp ground almonds
Vanilla essence
4 oz caster suger
Teacup sultanas
2 tbsp chopped walnuts
2 tbsp semolina
Smooth jam - any kind
Shortcrust pastry (using 4 oz flour if you are making it)

Line a 12 x 7 inch shallow tin with pastry, then spread the jam thinly over the base. Cream margarine and sugar. Add the egg, then the other ingredients and then spread over the jam on the pastry. Cook in a moderate oven, about 20 - 30 minutes, until the top is brown. Sprinkle with caster sugar when hot. Divide into squares.

Wendy Glover
Kent

Malt Bread

1 cup All Bran
½ cup dark brown sugar
Grated rind of a lemon
1 cup mixed dried fruit
Pinch mixed spice
1 cup milk

Mix ingredients and leave to stand for an hour. Add 1 cup of self raising flour and mix. Put all in greased loaf tin and bake at gas mark 3 for 1¼ hours. Delicious with or without butter.

Mrs Christopher Rowe
Sussex

Wholemeal Bread

6 oz plain flour
1 tsp baking soda
1½ oz margarine
¾ pt buttermilk
10 oz wholemeal flour
1 tsp salt
1 tbsp sugar

Mix all dry ingredients well, rub in margarine, mix in sugar, add buttermilk and mix in slowly. Leave for 5 minutes. Butter a 2 lb loaf tin and dust with flour. Put mix in tin and level top. Bake in the centre of a preheated oven, 400°F / 200°C / gas 6, for 45 minutes.

Mrs Ann Radford
Northern Ireland

Brownies

2 oz unsweetened chocolate and 2½ oz shortening
OR
2 oz cocoa mixed with 5 tbsp water and mixed to a cream and 3 oz shortening
2 eggs
3 oz flour
Pinch salt
8 oz sugar
½ tsp baking powder
4 oz shelled walnuts, chopped roughly

Set oven at 350°F / gas 4. Cut up chocolate and put in a saucepan with shortening over a gentle heat. Whisk eggs and sugar together until light. Add chocolate mixture. Sift flour with baking powder and salt and stir into mixture with wooden spoon. Stir in walnuts. Spread into prepared 8 inch square cake tin and bake for 30 - 35 minutes in pre-set oven, or until a "dull" crust has formed. Allow to cool slightly and cut into squares.

Anne Crossley
Norfolk

My Favourite Canadian Shortbread Tarts

1 cup butter (8 oz)
1½ cups flour (12 oz)
½ cup icing sugar (4 oz)
1 tbsp cornflour

Use tiny muffin tins approx 1½ inch diameter.

Mix all the ingredients together in a mixmaster. Don't roll but pat into muffin tins with your fingers to form shell. Prick the bottoms with a fork. Bake at 325°F for twenty minutes. During baking time prick the bottoms again if the shells puff up.

Anonymous

Welsh Cakes

8 oz SR flour
½ tsp mixed spice
2 oz caster sugar
1 medium egg
Pinch salt
4 oz butter / margarine / lard
3 - 4 oz currants
1 - 2 tbsp cold milk to mix

Sift flour, salt and mixed spice into a bowl. Rub in fat until mixture resembles fine bread crumbs. Mix to a stiff paste with egg and milk. Turn onto a floured board, knead lightly till smooth then roll out to ¼ inch thick. Cut 2½ inches round. Cook on well greased griddle, thick frying pan or hot plate allowing 1½ - 2 minutes per side. Serve cakes warm dusted with caster sugar.

James Lewis
London

Chocolate Rum Cake

Serves 12 - 14

8 oz butter
4 oz caster sugar
2 tbsp dark rum
8 oz plain sweet biscuits, roughly broken
4 oz mixed nuts, roughly chopped (walnuts, toasted almonds and hazelnuts)
4 oz Maraschino cherries, well drained or glacé
8 oz plain chocolate
3 eggs

Grease a 23 x 13 cm (9 x 5 inch) loaf tin and line the bottom with greaseproof paper. Melt butter and chocolate together in a saucepan over gentle heat. Allow to cool. Place the sugar and eggs in a bowl and whisk together until pale and thick. Fold in the chocolate mixture and then add the remaining ingredients. Spoon mixture into the prepared tin. Cover and freeze. To serve, unmould onto a serving plate and allow to soften in the fridge for about 30 minutes. Cut into slices and serve.

Cootchy Tennant
Kent

Australian Ice Cream Christmas Cake Pudding

Serves 10

Best made two days ahead and kept covered in freezer

2 tsp coffee powder
100 g dark chocolate, melted
300 ml double cream
1½ cups dried mixed fruit
½ cup chopped glacé cherries
1 tbsp hot water
2 eggs, lightly beaten
¾ cup dark rum
1 litre vanilla ice cream

Combine coffee and hot water in bowl, add chocolate, mix well then stir in the eggs. Beat cream until soft peaks form then fold it into the chocolate mixture. Gently stir in rum and mixed fruit. Pour mixture into a 20 cm ring mould, cover and freeze until firm. Soften ice cream, add cherries and pour over chocolate mixture. Cover and freeze again.

To serve:

Turn on to serving plate and wipe base of pan with a hot cloth to ease removal. Serve with cream, blueberries and a copious quantity of alcohol.

Jane Alliott
Japan

Patti's Ginger Things

8 oz self raising flour
2 - 3 oz soft brown sugar
1 tsp ginger
Pinch salt
4 oz margarine
½ tsp golden syrup
½ tsp bicarbonate of soda
3 oz dried fruit

Cream margarine and sugar together. Add syrup and the rest of the ingredients (dried fruit last). When blended press into a lined tin. Bake at gas 2 - 3 / 325°F / 160°C for 30 minutes. Allow to cool slightly in tin, then mark into squares and turn out gently.

Very easy, very good and will happily freeze.

Rosemary Raymond
Kent

Fruit Cake

8 oz margarine
12 oz self raising flour
4 eggs
4 oz mixed peel
8 oz sugar
1 tsp baking powder
1 lb sultanas
A little milk

Cream the fat and sugar. Add the beaten eggs alternately with the flour. Add the fruit and a little milk if necessary. Cook in an 8 or 10 inch cake tin for about 2 hours at gas 4 / 180°C for half an hour and then turn it down to gas 2 / 150°C for the rest of the cooking.

Mrs David Holman
Kent

Health Cakes

2 oz margarine
2 oz caster sugar
1 dstsp black treacle
1 heaped dstsp bran
2 oz self raising flour
1 egg warmed and slightly whisked
1 heaped tbsp sultanas
A little vanilla essence

Mix all ingredients together and put into 9 well greased and floured patty-tins. Make sure the oven is hot and cook for 17 minutes at gas 6 / 400°F / 200°C. Remove from tins while still warm.

Jane Smallwood
Kent

Christmas Cake (for nut lovers)

Mix together:

6 oz dried apricots cut up
6 oz whole hazel nuts
4 oz candied peel
2 oz glacé cherries
6 oz pecan nuts crushed (or walnuts)
6 oz raisins
2 oz macadamia nuts (or brazil)
4 oz banana chips (sweetened)

Whisk together:

4 oz plain flour
½ tsp baking powder
3 eggs
3 oz soft brown sugar
Juice and rind of a lemon

Mix it all together and put into parchment lined 2½ pt baba tin (so that middle gets cooked) and cover with parchment. Then cook 2 hours at 160°C / 325°F.

Barbara Spens
Kent

Lemon Bars

½ cup butter
¼ cup icing sugar
1 cup granulated sugar
¼ tsp salt
1 cup and 2 tbsp flour
2 eggs slightly beaten
3 tbsp lemon juice
Grated rind of 1 lemon

Mix together the butter, the cup of flour and the icing sugar - you can do this in a Magimix. Put this in an 8 inch square tin and press down with fingers to form an even layer crust. Bake for 15 minutes at 350°F. Mix eggs, granulated sugar, lemon juice and rind, salt and remaining flour. Pour over hot crust. Bake for 20 minutes. Cool and sieve over more icing sugar. Serve with a big glass of milk or a hot cup of tea or coffee.

Mrs James Woodhouse

Coffee Cake

4 oz soft margarine
2 tbsp coffee essence
6 oz soda bread flour
4 oz sugar
2 large eggs

1. Cream the sugar and margarine. Add coffee essence, egg and flour alternately.
2. Line an 8 inch cake tin and pour in the mix.
3. Bake for half an hour on gas 6 / 400°F / 200°C. Do not open the oven.

This recipe can also be used for a chocolate cake - change the coffee essence for drinking chocolate mixed with a little hot water.

Mrs Ann Radford
Northern Ireland

Mincemeat Cake

8 oz self raising flour
4 oz caster sugar
3 oz dried fruit (no cherries)
5 oz soft margarine
2 eggs
1 jar mincemeat

Mix all together and put it in a loaf tin. Bake for 1 hour at gas 4 / 360°F.

Alison Laughton
Kent

Guinness Loaf

8 oz (225 g) sultanas
6 fl oz Guinness or other stout
1 beaten egg
1 oz chopped whole blanched almonds
8 oz (225 g) self raising flour
4 oz (115 g) soft dark brown sugar

Soak the fruit overnight in the Guinness. Strain and keep the liquid. Mix all the ingredients and add the Guinness - a little extra may be needed, which you will have left, won't you, or did you think that bit left in the bottle was the cook's perk? Line the bottom of a 2 lb loaf tin with greased greaseproof paper. Spoon in the mixture. Bake in a pre-heated oven gas 4 / 350°F for 1 hour or until a metal skewer comes out clean. Turn out and allow to cool. Store in foil to keep moist. Slice thinly, spread with butter.

Mary Scanlon
Sligo, Ireland

15th Fairway Cake

A scrappy piece of paper found on the 15th fairway of Chart Hills golf course. Picking it up, thinking it to be litter, I found it to be a recipe. I took it home and made it - a delicious and dead easy cake. I like the golf course even more!

1 natural yoghurt (125ml) - use empty pot as measure for the sugar, flour & oil:
2 pots sugar
3 pots flour
1 pot oil
4 eggs
1 teaspoon baking powder
Add ½ - ¾ pot of rum (preferably Negrita)
Lastly add walnuts and sultanas (I used a handful of each!)
1 pint of best bitter

Put everything except nuts and fruit in food processor and whizz for 10 seconds. Add fruit and nuts and whizz for another few seconds. Cook at 170°C for about an hour or until brown and shrinking from sides of tin. I presume the best bitter was for the '19th Hole' rather than the 15th Fairway Cake!

Mrs David Spry
Kent

Passion Cake

225 g (8 oz) SR flour
Pinch salt
2 level tsp ground cinnamon
150 ml (¼ pt) vegetable oil
175 g (6 oz) carrots
2 ripe bananas
50 g (2 oz) icing sugar
Halved walnuts to decorate
2 tsp baking powder
150 g (5 oz) soft light brown sugar
2 eggs
50 g (2 oz) walnuts
1 lemon
125 g (4 oz) cream cheese
2 - 3 tbsp milk

Grease and base line 2 x 20 cm / 8 inch sandwich tins. Sift together flour, baking powder, salt, sugar and cinnamon. Beat the eggs and the oil together and blend in the dry ingredients. Grate the carrots, mash bananas and chop walnuts finely. Add carrots, banana and walnuts to mixture with the grated rind and juice of lemon. Blend well. Divide mixture between the two tins, smooth tops and bake 180°C / gas 4 for 35 minutes until well risen and golden. Cool on rack. To make icing - blend the cream cheese with the sieved icing sugar and enough milk to make a spreadable consistency. When cakes are cold, sandwich together with half the mixture. Spread the rest over the top and decorate with walnuts.

Jane Alvey
Sussex

Spiced Bread

10 oz self raising flour
½ tsp ground ginger
6 oz sultanas
2 oz margarine
1 large egg
½ tsp mixed spice
4 oz soft brown sugar
2 oz peel
6 tbsp milk
6 oz syrup

Sieve all dry ingredients. Add sugar, peel and fruit. Melt margarine and syrup gently. Do not boil. Stir in dry ingredients. Beat egg and milk and stir into mixture. Pour into 2 lb loaf tin. Cook for 1½ hours gas 3 / 325°F.

Mrs Ben Wright
Kent

Cheese and Tomato Bread

This recipe makes 2 good sized loaves - one can be frozen!

Cheese and tomato bread is a scrumptious (and spectacular) accompaniment to a bowl of good home-made soup. You will be delighted by the look of surprise on the faces of your guests when you cut into the loaf and they see the swirl of tomato inside the cheese bread. It is also delicious toasted and served with scrambled or poached eggs as a light supper. Toasted and spread with anchovy paste or Gentlemen's Relish it makes an unusual and tasty cocktail snack. I am sure that once you have found how easy this bread is to make and just how good it tastes you will find many different ways to serve it.

Have 2 mixing bowls ready with 1½ lb of strong plain white flour in each.

Bowl A - Cheese:

Add

1 sachet fast action dried yeast
10 oz strong Cheddar cheese - grated
10 tbsp olive oil
½ tsp sugar
1 level dstsp salt
½ tsp cayenne pepper
1 pt warm water

Mix all these ingredients together using the dough hook on the electric mixer - or with a wooden spoon and then kneading by hand - until the dough is smooth - approx 5 minutes. Stand it aside (out of any draughts) with an oiled paper over the top of the dough and then a clean cloth over the top of the bowl until the dough has doubled in size, (approx 1 hour).

Bowl B - Tomato:

Add

1 sachet fast action dried yeast
8 tbsp olive oil
1 tbsp dried basil (or other herb)
1 level dstsp salt
½ tsp sugar
4 rounded tbsp tomato purée
½ pt or just over, warm water to mix with the tomato purée

Prepare in exactly the same manner as Bowl A. When both doughs have risen well, take the cheese dough out first, lightly knead on a floured board and cut into 2 equal portions - put to one side whilst you deal with the tomato dough in exactly the same manner.

Take one of the pieces of cheese dough and roll out into a rectangle approximately a quarter of an inch thick - then roll out one of the pieces of tomato dough until it is the same size. Put the tomato dough on top of the cheese dough and roll up like a swiss roll. Put into a well greased loaf tin - or place onto a flat baking sheet. Cover with a cloth. Treat the other 2 pieces of dough in the same way. Leave to rise for 20 minutes. Brush with olive oil and sprinkle with finely grated Parmesan cheese. If you have a traditional oven - heat oven to 450°F / 230°C / gas 8. Bake loaves at this temp for 20 minutes, reduce heat to 400°F / 200°C / gas 6 for another 20 minutes. The loaves are cooked if they sound hollow when you tap the bottom - if they don't sound hollow put them back into the oven for another 5 minutes. With a fan assisted oven the loaves can be put in while the oven is still cold. Turn oven to 200°C and after 20 minutes, reduce to 180°C for another 20 minutes. Treat as above.

These loaves freeze very well. If you have only used half the loaf, cut the rest into slices ready for toasting - freeze - these can then be used singly as required, leaving the other slices to be used as needed in the future.

As this is quite an extravagant recipe for bread it can be made using half the quantities used above, should the housekeeping be running a bit low.

Edna Harrisson
Kent

Afghan Biscuits

7 oz butter
2 oz cornflakes
6 oz plain flour
½ tsp vanilla essence
3 oz sugar
Walnuts to decorate
1 level tbsp cocoa

Cream the butter and sugar together. Add other ingredients and mix together. Place spoonfuls on greased baking tray. Bake for 15 - 20 minutes in moderate oven (180°C). Ice with chocolate icing and decorate with walnut pieces.

Mrs Glen Meyer
Auckland NZ

Mincemeat Shortcake

½ cup caster sugar
1 egg
2 cups flour
1 tsp vanilla essence or grated rind and juice of ½ lemon
Mincemeat, apple sauce or jam
4 oz butter (not marg!)
2½ rounded tsp baking powder

Cream butter and sugar, add lightly beaten egg and vanilla or lemon. Sift in dry ingredients to make soft dough. Chill quarter of the dough in fridge or freezer. Spread the rest of the dough over base of greased 9 inch round cake tin or 13 x 9 inch sponge tin. Base should not be too thick. Mincemeat, apple or jam on top. Then grate hardened dough coarsely over top to cover mincemeat. Bake about 40 minutes at 350°F until golden on surface. Cut when cold.

Mrs David Fowler

Toffee and Almond Slices

For the pastry:

125 g unsalted butter
250 g sieved plain flour
125 g sieved icing sugar
1 egg (size 3)

For the almond topping:

100 g unsalted butter
100 g caster sugar
160 g flaked almonds
60 g honey
60 ml whipping cream

For the pastry:

In a bowl, sieve the flour and icing sugar. Mix in small pieces of the butter and work together using fingers until a sandy texture is reached. Mix in the egg and work to a smooth dough. Wrap in clingfilm and refrigerate for 1 hour. Lightly grease a 12 × 8 inch shallow baking tin. Roll out the pastry a quarter of an inch thick and line the baking tin. Prick the pastry with a fork and bake in a preheated oven - 200°C / gas 6 for around 7 - 10 minutes, until golden-brown. Leave to cool.

For the topping:

Place all the ingredients except the almonds into a saucepan and gently bring to a boil. When a light caramel colour is reached, remove from the heat and mix in the almond flakes. Spread this mixture evenly over the cooked pastry base and leave to cool. When cool cut into slices and serve. This will keep up to 4 or 5 days in an airtight container.

The Marchioness of Tavistock

Walnut Bread

1 lb 100% wholemeal flour
1 pkt Harvest Gold Fast Action yeast
1 dstsp salt
1 tbsp warmed molasses
Approximately ¾ pint tepid water
½ lb strong white flour
1 heaped teaspoon curry powder
1 oz margarine
2 ozs broken walnuts

1. Rub the fat into the flours in a bowl.
2. Add salt, curry powder and yeast. Mix well.
3. Make a well in the centre and pour in molasses.
4. Add half the water and mix with a wooden spoon; gradually add more water and use hands to work into a cohesive lump of dough.
5. Knead well for 5 to 10 minutes (or 3 minutes with an electric mixer dough hook).
6. Cover the bowl with a plastic bag and leave to rise in a cold place until doubled in size. If the rising is too warm the bread will have less flavour.
7. Punch down the dough and add the walnuts. Shape into 2 plaits and put on a greased baking sheet.
8. Prove in a warm place and cover with plastic again for 20 - 30 minutes or until well risen.
9. Glaze with a beaten egg if desired.
10. Bake at 400°F / gas 6 for 20 minutes, then reduce to 375°F / gas 5 for a further 20 minutes.

The cooked loaves should sound hollow when tapped on the base.

Patricia Jacobs
Extract from "Bread Wholesome Bread"

Mini Macaroon Biscuits

Serves 6

3 egg whites
150 g / 6 oz caster sugar
100 g / 4 oz chopped slivered almonds

1. Heat the oven to 100°C / 200°F.
2. Line a baking tray with non-stick baking paper. Brush over with melted butter.
3. Whip up the egg whites until they are stiff. Fold in the sugar and then the almonds. Pipe with a large nozzle onto the baking tray and bake for 20 to 30 minutes. Turn onto a cake rack to cool.

Mrs Beverley Parker
Kent

Saucepan Cake

½ 1b fairly plain biscuits
4 oz cooking chocolate
2 oz butter
2 tbsp golden syrup

Crush the biscuits. Melt together the butter, chocolate and golden syrup in a small saucepan over a low heat and stir in crumbled biscuits. If desired glacé cherries, glacé ginger, raisins or coconut can be added. Put into an oiled tin. Press in firmly and smooth over with a cut orange.

This cake will keep (if the family does not find it) for some weeks if wrapped firmly in kitchen foil.

Mrs Olive McGregger

Chocolate Chip Cookies

4 oz butter
2 oz granulated sugar
3 oz brown sugar
1 egg
½ tsp vanilla essence
4 oz plain flour
½ tsp bicarb of soda
½ tsp salt
4 oz choc broken into little bits

Cream butter and sugars until light and fluffy, add egg and vanilla essence. Fold in flour, bicarb and salt. Then add choc bits. Spoon heaped teaspoons of mixture onto greased baking sheets. they tend to spread so leave some room! Cook until light and brown about 10 minutes, try not to overcook as they go rather hard then soft and chewy. Remove cookies from tray while still hot and leave to cool, when they crisp up. Make lots as they are very yummy.

Fiona Hughes D'Aeth
Dorset

Orange - Rhubarb Breakfast Cake

Makes one 13 by 9 inch cake

1/3 cup sugar
½ cup finely chopped walnuts
1 tsp cinnamon
2/3 cup vegetable oil
1 egg
2¼ cups all-purpose flour
1 tsp baking soda
2 cups rhubarb, cut into ½ inch pieces
1 tbsp unsalted butter, softened
1½ tsp finely grated orange zest
1 1/3 cups (packed) light brown sugar
1 cup buttermilk
1 tsp vanilla extract
¼ cup oat-bran
Pinch of salt
1 tbsp confectioners sugar

1. Preheat the oven to 350°F. Lightly butter a 13 × 9 inch baking pan.
2. In a small bowl, using your fingers rub the sugar and butter together until blended. Mix in the walnut and half teaspoon each of the orange zest and cinnamon. Set the strudel topping aside.
3. In a large bowl, blend the brown sugar and oil. Add the buttermilk, egg and vanilla and stir to combine. In a medium bowl, toss the flour, oatbran, baking soda, salt and remaining one teaspoon orange zest and half teaspoon cinnamon. Stir the dry ingredients into the buttermilk mixture until combined, fold in the rhubarb.
4. Spoon the batter into the prepared pan. Sprinkle the reserved strudel topping over the top. Bake for about 50 minutes, or until a cake tester (!) inserted in the centre of the cake comes out clean. Let cool on a rack for at least 10 minutes. Sift the confectioners sugar on top and serve.

Mrs Anthony Talbot
New York

Brown Soda Bread

675 g / 1½ 1b brown wholemeal flour
450 g / 1 1b white flour
30 g / 1 oz fine oatmeal
30 g / 1 oz butter
1 egg beaten
10 g / 2 rounded teaspoon salt
10 g / 2 rounded teaspoons bread soda, sieved
730 - 860 ml / 1¼ - 1½ pints sour milk or buttermilk

Heat your oven to 230°C / 450°F / gas 8.

Thoroughly mix all the flour, salt, soda and oatmeal, then rub in all the butter. Make a well in the middle, add the beaten egg then most of the sour milk or butter milk. Mix (hands are the best!) adding more milk if necessary to produce a soft but not sticky dough. Turn on to a floured board and knead lightly into a round shape about 3 inch / 8 cm high. Put on a baking sheet, cut a deep cross in the top of the dough and bake at 230°C / 450°F / gas 8 for 20 minutes. Reduce heat to 200°C / 400°F / gas 6 and bake for a further 20 - 25 minutes until the bread is cooked and hollow-sounding when tapped.

Serve with Kerrygold butter of course! Delicious for afternoon tea with a cup of Earl Grey and strawberry jam, or for breakfast with marmalade or Marmite.

Mrs Michael Opperman
Worcestershire

Gingerbread

This is a recipe handed down to the 3rd generation of ex Ashford School Girls which I thought you might like for "Absolutely Delicious". Not very exciting but a recipe which was used in the school in about the 1920s.

14 oz SR flour
4 oz butter
8 oz brown sugar
1 tsp ground ginger
2 tsp cinnamon
1 tsp mixed spice
1 tsp bicarbonate soda
2 tbsp black treacle
1 tbsp golden syrup
1 fresh egg
1 teacup milk

Melt black treacle, syrup, butter and milk in a saucepan and stir into dry ingredients. Put into square meat tin and bake for 1 hour in a slow oven, gas 2½ / 320°F / 155°C.

Mrs John Ash
Kent

Classic Fruit Cake

9 oz self raising flour
6 oz brown sugar
Grated rind of one orange
4 eggs
6 oz butter or margarine
3 oz cherries
1 1b mixed fruit
1½ tablespoons milk

Rub together the fat and flour and then stir in the other ingredients in turn. Turn into a greased and lined 2 1b loaf tin and bake for 2 hours in the centre of the oven at gas 2 / 290°F.

The recipe can be varied by substituting different fruits and nuts, I have made it with prunes and apricots, and by using part wholemeal flour, and using a spirit in place of milk.

Rose Lewis

Tea Brack

Makes 1 good sized loaf

12 oz sultanas
5 fl oz strong cold tea
2½ oz self raising flour
4 oz brown sugar
1 egg

Add sultanas and sugar to cold tea and leave overnight. Next day, beat egg and add to sultana mixture. Sift in flour. Put mixture into a greased and floured loaf tin. Bake slowly for 1½ hours. Test with knitting needle to make sure it is done. Leave to cool in tin, then turn out, slice and spread with lashings of butter!

Mrs Ian Johnston
Kent

Spiced Carrot Cake Tray Bake

4 oz butter
1 egg
4 level tbsp marmalade
2 tbsp orange juice
8 oz self raising flour
2 oz walnuts, roughly chopped
6 oz caster sugar
1 level tsp mixed spice
Grated rind of one orange
Pinch salt
8 oz grated raw carrot

Line the cake tin with silicone paper. Cream the butter and sugar, add eggs, mixed spice, marmalade, orange rind and juice. Beat till well blended. Mix the salt in flour, toss carrots and walnuts in flour to coat them to prevent sinking. Add carrot mix to rest of ingredients, turn into prepared tin. Bake at 160°C for 35 - 40 minutes. Cool in tin.

Icing:

3 level tbsp of fine shred marmalade
4 oz sifted icing sugar

Mix together in bowl over warm water. Spread over cake. Allow to set, then cut into slices.

Ros Martin
Kent

Lemon Top Cake

A particular favourite with the girls at Ashford School in the 1990s.

100 g wholemeal S R flour
100 g soft margarine
2 eggs
1 level tsp baking powder
100 g caster sugar

Topping:

½ lemon
50 g caster sugar

1. Light oven gas 5 / 190°C. Place shelf in centre. Grease 7 inch square cake tin.
2. Sieve flour and baking powder into a bowl. Add rest of the ingredients and beat well with a wooden spoon or electric mixer for 5 minutes.

3. Turn into the prepared tin and bake for 20 - 30 minutes until golden brown and firm.
4. Meanwhile, prepare topping - squeeze juice from lemon and place in a small basin with caster sugar. Stir until sugar has dissolved.
5. When cake is cooked remove from oven and brush all the topping over cake. Leave to cool in tin before cutting into squares.

Ginny Lingwood
Ashford School

Queen Mother's Favourite Cake

Cake:

1 breakfast cup boiling water
1 tsp bicarbonate of soda
10 oz flour
2 oz chopped nuts (pecan or walnut)
½ tsp salt
1 tsp vanilla
8 oz chopped dates
3 oz butter / marg
8 oz sugar
1 tsp baking powder
1 egg

Pour the boiling water over the dates, add the bicarbonate of soda and let it stand. Rub the butter into the flour and add the sugar, nuts, baking powder and salt. Beat the egg with the vanilla and add to the butter mixture. Add the date mixture and stir well. Bake in a buttered, greaseproof 9 x 9 inch tin for 45 minutes at 375°F.

Icing:

7½ tbsp dark brown sugar
3 oz butter
3 tbsp cream or top of milk

Melt slowly and allow to boil for 3 - 4 minutes stirring well. Allow to cool and thicken and pour over the cake.

Mrs Walter Gilson
S Africa

Chocolate Marshmallow Cake

7 oz plain flour
2 oz cocoa
10 oz caster sugar
3 eggs
1 tsp baking powder
A pinch of salt
8 oz soft margarine
1 tsp vanilla essence
4 oz chocolate chips
4 oz marshmallows (small American white ones are best)

1. Preheat oven to 180°C / 350°F / gas 4.
2. Line a 13 x 9 inch tin with silver foil.
3. Sift together the dry ingredients by mixing for about 15 seconds in a food processor.
4. Mix in all other ingredients. (Be careful it does not spill out of the top of your processor!)
5. Blend for about 30 seconds or until the ingredients are well mixed.
6. Spread in the tin.
7. Bake for 25 minutes exactly, (20 minutes in a fan oven). It may look a little underdone when you take it out but the trick is not to let the top 'catch' as then it will dry out and be too hard. The consistency of the cake is quite moist and chewy. Leave in the tin for 10 minutes before turning it out onto a cooling rack. Wait until it is cool before removing the silver foil and cutting into squares.

Anne Gould
Ashford School

Christmas Fruit Cake

1 cup water
4 large eggs
1 tsp salt
1 cup brown sugar
Juice of one lemon
1 cup sugar
2 cups dried fruit
1 tsp baking soda
8 oz nuts
1 bottle of whisky

Sample the whisky to check for quality.

Take a large bowl. Check the whisky again. To be sure it is of the highest quality, pour one level cup and drink. Repeat.

Turn on the electric mixer, beat one cup of butter in a large fluffy bowl. add one tsp, sugar and beat again. Make sure the whisky is still okay. Try another tup. Turn off the mixerer. Break two eggs and add to the bowl and chuck in the dried fruit. Mix on the turner.

If the fried druit gets stuck in the beaterers, pry it loose with a drewscriver.Sample the whisky to check for tonsisticity.
Next sift two cups of salt. Or something. Who cares?Check the whisky.
Now sift the lemon juice and strain your nuts. Add on table. Spoon. Of sugar or something. Whatever you can find. Grease the oven. Turn the cake tin to 350 degrees. Don't forget to beat off the turner. Throw the bowl out of the window, check the whisky again and go to bed!*Biddy Boucher*

Kent

INDEX TO ABSOLUTELY DELICIOUS

INDEX TO ABSOLUTELY DELICIOUS

INDEX TO ABSOLUTELY DELICIOUS

INDEX TO ABSOLUTELY DELICIOUS

INDEX TO ABSOLUTELY DELICIOUS

INDEX TO ABSOLUTELY DELICIOUS

INDEX TO ABSOLUTELY DELICIOUS

Cover photograph courtesy of:
Brake Bros. Foodservice Ltd. and Larderfresh